Apostle De Burney

What CHRIST Did for You to Make You Right with God

"AFTER The CROSS"

RIGHTEOUSNESS OF CHRIST CHURCH

CHRIST HAS RISEN

RIGHTEOUSNESS OF CHRIST

What Christ Did

To Make You Right with God

"After the Cross"

Taught through God's Scriptures!

HOW many books have you read where the scriptures themselves give you the answers to Biblical questions and not the commentary of the Author?

A Book that uses the Word of God to interpret the Word of God!

<u>There is some commentary in here to help you understand what</u>

<u>Christ has done for You *"After The Cross."*</u>

<u>However, I believe the best descriptions and answers to the Bible and Biblical Questions are through the Bible itself.</u>

<u>So, most of what you will be reading are answers to Spiritual questions about What Christ did *"After The Cross"* and they will come from the Word of God!</u>

"TAKING IT FROM THE CHURCH TO THE STREET'S"

Me

Table of Contents

Acknowledgments

I give thanks to:

- **God,** first, who inspired me to write this book. Through **Jesus Christ,** He gave me the wisdom and strength to walk in His Righteousness and not my own.

- **My Family:** Father Alvin Wakefield, Mrs. Rose Wakefield, Sister Dana, and Lesley Wakefield.

- My wife, **Prophetess Belinda Burney;** she allowed me to grow in God without hindrances and stood by my side all the way. I Love You Very Much!

- **All My Children,** Latice Greene, Thenisha Greene, Darius Greene, Derrick Brookins, Derricca Burney, and Chantille Burney. Then God brought Kaleen Hollins and Lauren Moore and Christopher Ruffins (R.I.P.). You all are the blessings God gave to me. I am so proud and grateful that God gave you to me. **I LOVE YOU ALL WITH EVERYTHING IN ME!**

- My sister, **Roberta Lowery;** she has truly supported me through the ministry, with love for her "Big Brother" like no other.

Through the immortal words of Gee Money, "We all we Got!" we are the eldest of our family tree line; the rest of them has gone to heaven.

- My **Pastor/Bishop Sharon Moore** who taught the Word of God and the spiritual things of the Word of God. She ordained me as a minister, then Pastor. Thank you so much for putting up with me all those years and grooming me to be used by God.

- My **Bishop/Apostle Gregory Holley and Pastor Diane Holley** who ordained me as an Apostle and taught me how to serve the people in the community and on the streets, and to draw souls to the Lord.

"Faith without Works is Dead."

AND to **My ROCC FAMILY,** you are the blessing God gave me to watch over. I Love All of You Very Much! Thank You All for being a part of the "Righteousness of Christ Church Ministries."

- And **Honorable Mentions,** you all have been special in my Walk with the Lord this season: *Bishop* **W.F. Bridges**, *Bishop* **Phil Brownlee**, *Apostle* **Glynis Thomas**, *Pastor* **Edward & Deborah Cook**, Minister **Glen & Dawn Thomas.** Also, **Tyrone Spencer** (who gave me some spiritual help).

And my R.O.C.C. Ministries Family: I LOVE YOU ALL.

- *Pastor* **Sylvester Garth** (**God** used you to give me my start on this new **spiritual** journey He set before me when all these relationships started. I am forever grateful. **Thank You!**).

- **My Family who are in heaven;** Grandfather Floyd Burney, Granny Hattie Burney, Mother Ruth Burney, Willie Burney, Brother Atremus Doss. Son, Christopher Ruffins.

The Author's Story
[Apostle De Burney]

Apostle De Burney is the pastor of Righteousness of Christ Church (R.O.C.C.) Ministries. He is a graduate with two bachelor's degrees from Fontbonne University, and a seminary degree—a Master's in Divinity—from Liberty University. Apostle De Burney now devotes his time to teaching people to live the GOSPEL that Jesus gave Paul to PREACH. He teaches them to be free from the LAW and how to live in the Righteousness of Christ, so God can use them to be His disciples without CONDEMNATION, by accepting what Christ has done for THEM (Romans 8:1-4).

This book is about setting people free from the law and raising them back up into the Righteousness of Christ (**After the Cross**) through scriptures. He searched and was not able to find scriptures to defend the Righteousness of God's belief systems till God revealed them to him (**Eph. 3:8-10 NKJV**).

Most people leave Christ at the Cross and do not receive what He has done for them beyond salvation, therefore, they cannot live a life free from bondage! God told him when he started the church, "You are not building a church. You are building disciples." Presently, Apostle De Burney is now being used by God to teach them how they can be of use by God. This book, *The Righteousness of Christ "After the Cross,"* will set you free from the law, bondage, and condemnation so you can live a life free in Christ Jesus!

Apostle De Burney shows how to become Disciples of Christ by allowing the Holy Spirit to teach us how to love God and accept what CHRIST has done for us. Then we can be taught by the Holy Spirit on how to live right and work for God (**Titus 2:12 niv**) Apostle De Burney's ministry is materialized through the guidance of the Holy Spirit to go about helping out in the community, (not just their own community) by feeding, clothing, praying, and opening the door for Salvation to the people so God can draw them into the Kingdom of Heaven. His church also helps other churches with their community outreach needs through physical services.

One day, his sister called him and said that she and her husband had free tickets to see Creflo Dollar. He remembered that his brother used to listen to Creflo Dollar when he started living for God. Therefore, he decided to go. He asked Belinda Ruffin (who later became his wife) to join him. When he got there, the Holy Spirit guided him to ask Belinda to give him a pen and paper, because God was going to set him free (which God did). He used Creflo Dollar to show him the Righteousness of God through the scriptures, and at that very moment, he was set free—never to be bound again by the laws. Creflo gave him four scriptures. When he got home, he studied what Creflo Dollar had taught him. God gave him four pages of scriptures, and he has been free from the law ever since through the Righteousness of Christ.

Satan has tricked some churches into believing that the way to God is through teaching people Moses' laws. However, 1 Timothy 1: 6-7 says they understand "neither what they say nor affirm" that they desire to be teachers of the law. Paul says that they are under a curse if they continue in the works of the law (**Galatians 3:10-12**). God says they have not accepted His Righteousness because they are trying to establish their own righteousness

(**Romans 10:3**). Paul said that he had to give up his righteousness by the law to accept God's way of making him right (**Philippians 3: 9**). Finally, the Bible says that Christ is the end of the law for Righteousness, for everyone that believes (**Romans 10:4**). Therefore, anyone trying to be right with God by the law is not following biblical principles because the law is not good for righteousness (**Romans 3:20**).

How the Righteousness of Christ was revealed to him by God?

Together with his siblings, Apostle De Burney was raised in church all his life by his mother, Ruth Burney, and grandmother, Hattie Burney. These two women taught his sister, Roberta; brother, Artemus; and him about God at an early age. At the age of 25, he moved out of his mother's house. Since he had been raised as a Christian, he never missed going to church. Even though he had the Christian faith, he found it hard to abide by the Bible's commandments. This made him live a sinful life and spent most of it trying to be right with God. When he was twelve years old and his brother was six, the deacon at the church, New White Stone Missionary Bible Church, prophesied to his mother that his brother and he would become preachers. That prophecy came true thirty years later.

He had not talked to his brother for about two years, and his sister came to him one day and told him that his brother was going to be preaching at a church on that Sunday and asked if he wanted to attend the service. He was in awe because his brother was truly a bad apple. "How did he end up becoming a preacher?" Apostle curiously asked himself as he attended the church. He believes that's when God started changing his life after he took a decision to change. While in the church, he made a silent prayer to God pleading with him to change who he was, just as God had done with his brother. That was the beginning of his transformation.

He wanted to know which Pastor was responsible for changing his brother's life and bringing him close to God. Upon inquiry, he found out that it was Sharon Moore, the Pastor of Church of Jesus Christ Kings of Kings and Lord of Lords. With this knowledge and the motivation of changing, he began going to her church. He believes that's when his life began to change. One thing that he liked about her was that she was not like the other pastors he had grown up knowing. She did not claim to be perfect. It wasn't till after he started going to her church that he was able to understand the meaning of Grace. This happened at a certain time she asked him to give a testimony in one of the church services. He declined her request on the basis that he had been living a sinful life, and hence was not a clean person. He stated he would never forget what her response was. In her exact words, she said, "You'll live for the world. Now God is asking you to work for Him, and you're now going to say no?" She continued, "God will clean you up, and you have to give Him a chance." Joining pastor Sharon's church gave him the opportunity to learn about God's Words and the spiritual aspects of God's Word.

Apostle Burney had always been taught that to be right with God, you had to start by keeping all His commandments. He thought that it was possible for an individual to live a perfect life as the pastors tried to set a good example by living the best life they could for God. Apostle always questioned himself why he was not living a perfect life that is free of sins. When he joined Pastor Sharon's church, he saw something different. He experienced grace even in his sinful state. This started his transformation from the law, into the righteousness of God.

The transformational journey began when he critically analyzed the message that was put out there to the congregation by Pastor Joseph Prince. Joseph believed that individuals did not have to work to be right with God. In his sermons, he would repeatedly say that individuals were not under the Law, a statement that made me think that he was giving false teaching and was hypocritical. He wondered where the Bible scriptures were that supported such an argument. To find out the truth, he studied the scriptures for six months while listening to Joseph Prince's sermons. He could not find anything to back him up, so he did not believe him at all, and he stayed bound in the law. The Bible teaches us that God has kept Christ hidden from some, and only revealed Him to those He willed to make known (**Colossians 1:26-27**). Then, Apostle De Burney knew he was one of those He kept it hidden from and did not will to make it known to at that time...

QUESTIONS

1. Has the Righteousness of Christ been revealed to you yet?

_____

_____

_____

2. Do you really understand what that means and what Christ has really done for you, "After the Cross"?

_____

_____

_____

Colossians 1:26-27 (NKJV)

The mystery, which has been hidden from ages and from generations, but now, has been revealed to His saints. To them God willed to make known what the riches of the glory of this mystery among the Gentiles are: which is Christ in you, the hope of glory.

Introduction

God's book on Righteousness is your everyday companion. This book can be used as a guide on teaching you what Christ has done for you. The information contained herein can help change the life of an individual. Those who accept Christ in their lives allow the Holy Spirit to teach them how to live a spiritual and righteous life. It is important to note that you can read this book in small groups as a Bible Study guide, something that could be facilitated as "The Righteousness of Christ" Book Study Guide. This is not a book in which I dictate a certain way of life, which as a Christian, you must strictly follow.

Rather, this book only gives guidelines of what entails of a righteous life, according to the teachings of Christ and His apostles. This book has been inspired by God's desire to shine light in the lives of some misinformed Christians, who are seeking to find the way. By reading this book, your relationship with Christ will develop to a higher level, and you will notice that you can find peace and freedom in a world full of struggles.

It will also answer some of the hardest questions that Christians face in their daily lives; for example, how to live through temptations, how to know when your work in Christ is paying off and when you are working in vain, and how to abide in Christ's love without being bound by the condemnation of the Law.

I recommend it for both strong believers in Christ and those who are in their first stage of Christianity. For the believers, it will strengthen their faith and remind them of what Christ has done for them beyond the Cross. Also, it will remind them of their purpose as Christians. It will lead them away from temptation and show them the right direction. For those still taking baby steps in Christianity, it will be a good start, which shows them all the essentials of accepting what Christ has done for them beyond the Cross and living a righteous life as a Christian.

What do you Gain by Reading this Book?

Every teaching and recommendations given in this book are in reference to the Bible. This work will, therefore, not only serve as your daily guide, but it will also motivate you to read the Bible more. It also gives contextual interpretations of the Bible and relates the historical context to today's context. We find that sometimes while reading the Bible, the true meaning of the scriptures is not registered in our minds. This book helps us understand the Bible in our current context. As you read the book,

- You will discover the real value of Christ's death on the Cross.

- You will discover what it means to love one another, forgive one another, and serve God wholeheartedly.

- It will help you to find out whether you are working towards something for God or just working in vain?

- You will discover whether you are walking in the Spirit or just following your instinct—which is dangerous, by the way!

- You will also learn a lot about what it means to live a righteous life through Christ, to forgive and love one another just as Christ loves us.

- You will be able to differentiate between being righteous by law or being righteous from what Christ has done for you "After the Cross."

Once you understand and accept what Christ did for you to make you right with God, you will release the Holy Spirit's authority to help you live a righteous life for God, without the condemnation that comes from making mistakes.

THE LAW IS STILL GOOD, BUT IT'S NOT FOR RIGHTEOUSNESS!

You cannot be right with God by keeping the law! You cannot be right with God by works of your own! Christ alone makes you right with God! (John 6:63; NLT)

Finally, how did the church come up with the name, Righteousness of Christ Church (R.O.C.C.) Ministries.

The name was given before the church was started but has undergone some transformation. While under Pastor Sharon Moore, the name was "Church of Jesus Christ Three, Wisdom Ministries." At the time the name was created, I had no ambition to pastor a church.

The name was gotten from suggestions Pastor Moore asked each member to make. Two years later, God told me to start a church, and He did something great within five weeks of this revelation. The church was started in the basement, and it kept the name for about a year and a half. One Sunday, the name was changed after God told me to pronounce to the congregation that August would be a month of new beginnings for the church. Then God produced a miracle, giving the church new furniture that same August.

By the last days of the month of August, I went into a chapel with a friend, Keven Porter. There the Chaplin said that the building was on its last day, as it would soon be demolished. He asked, "Do you know anyone who needs a podium, some pews, velvet chairs, books, and an organ?" I replied that I knew of such a person. This opened the way for God to fill the church with all those unexpected blessings. This was when God told me to change the name to "Wisdom Ministries 3." The name Wisdom came from Proverbs. Proverbs 8:1 says, "Does not wisdom cry out, and understanding lift up her voice?" Then there is Proverbs 8:35-36, which speaks of Jesus without mentioning His name. Wisdom is Jesus in those passages. The Bible states, "For whoever finds me finds life." In addition, Proverbs 9:1 says, "Wisdom has built her house" and gives us instructions of Wisdom. Likewise, Jesus gives us instruction for salvation. John 5:39 says, "You search the Scriptures, for in them you think you have eternal life; and these are they which testify of Me." That was how the name Wisdom came about, and God told me that I would put multiple disciples into churches from God. The number 3 equals the Father, Son, and the Holy Spirit.

God is changing the name again one last time to R.O.C.C.

Ministries is another story on its own. Jesus is the foundation, "On this rock, I will build my church" (R.O.C.C. – *Righteousness of Christ Church Ministries*). You must have the Wisdom of Christ before you can build His church, with Him as a foundation. Psalms 127:1 says, "Unless the LORD builds the house, they labor in vain who build it." God sent Christ to build the foundation for you to have a relationship with Him. Tie that into Proverbs 9:1 and you will see "Wisdom has built her house." The word, "Wisdom," represents Christ. First Corinthians 3:11 says, "For no other foundation can anyone lay than that which is laid, which is JESUS CHRIST." The main focus of my teaching is Christ and what Christ has done for you "After the Cross."

Are Jews and Gentiles both entitled to the Benefits of Christ?

Yes, they are!!!

Galatians 3:14-18 (NKJV):

(Christ ties Gentiles to the Blessings of Abraham)

14 That the blessing of Abraham might come upon the Gentiles in Christ Jesus, that we might receive the promise of the Spirit through faith.

The Changeless Promise

15 Brethren, I speak in the manner of men: Though it is only a man's covenant, yet if it is confirmed, no one annuls or adds to it. 16Now to Abraham and his Seed were the promises made. He does not say, "And to seeds," as of many, but as of one, "And to your Seed," who is Christ. 17And this I say, that the law, which was four hundred and thirty years later, cannot annul the covenant that was confirmed before by God in Christ, that it should make the promise of no effect. 18For if the inheritance is of the law, it is no longer of promise; but God gave it to Abraham by promise.

Galatians 3:29 (NKJV):

(The Gentiles are Abraham Seed and are heirs to his Blessings)

29And if you are Christ's, then you are Abraham's seed, and heirs according to the promise.

Galatians 3:28 (NIV)

(Neither Jew nor Gentile; we are all one)

[28]*There is neither Jew nor Gentile, neither slave nor free, nor is there male and female, for you are all one in Christ Jesus.*

Ephesians 2:14-20 (NLT)

(Christ created for Himself One New People from Two Groups—Jews and Gentiles; together as One Body, He reconciled them to God)

[14] *For Christ himself has brought peace to us. He United Jews and Gentiles into ONE People when, in his own body on the cross, he broke down the wall of hostility that separated us.* [15] *He did this by **ending the System of Law** with its commandments and regulations. **He made peace between Jews and Gentiles** by creating in himself **ONE New People from the Two Groups.*** [16] ***Together as one body, Christ reconciled both groups to God by means of His Death on The CROSS,** and our hostility toward each other was put to death.*

[17] *He brought this Good News of peace to you Gentiles who were far away from him, and peace to the Jews who were near.* [18] *Now all of us can come to the Father through the same Holy Spirit because of what Christ has done for us.*

A Temple for the Lord

[19] *So now you Gentiles are no longer strangers and foreigners. **You are citizens along with all of God's holy people.** You are members of God's family.* [20] *Together, we are his house, built on the foundation of the apostles and the prophets. And the cornerstone is Christ Jesus himself.*

Now that we know Jews and Gentiles are entitled to the work that Christ did "After the Cross," let's begin to study Christ's work "After the Cross."

Chapter 1
Has the Church Been Lifting Up Jesus?

John 12:32-36 (NKJV)

³²And I, if I am lifted up from the earth, I will draw all peoples to Myself.

Let no one trick you into not lifting up Christ. Be careful, because they will have you lifting up regulations and the law instead!

Colossians 2:18, Romans 10:4

¹⁸Let No man beguile you of your rewards. And ⁴Christians are not under the law to be right with God.

People will deceive you through their conducts. Those that do not live their lives based on the principles of what Jesus wants for you or what He has done for you, they will keep you under works as you try to be right with God with vain deception and sometimes with good intentions. However, if you take this position and don't build your foundation on what Christ has done for you, you will be working in vain and you will lose your rewards.

Psalms 127:1 (NKJV):

"Unless the LORD builds the house, they labor in vain who build it."

1 Corinthians 3:10-15 (NKJV)

[10] *According to the grace of God, which was given to me, as a wise master builder I have laid the foundation, and other builds on it. But let each one take heed how he **builds on it**. [11] For no other foundation can anyone lay than that which is laid, **which is Jesus Christ**. [12] Now if anyone builds on this foundation with gold, silver, precious stones, wood, hay, straw, [13] each one's work will become clear; for the Day will declare it, because it will be revealed by fire; and the fire will test each one's work, of what sort it is. [14] If anyone's work which he has built on it endures, he will receive a reward. [15] If anyone's work is burned, he will suffer loss; but he himself will be saved, yet so as through fire.*

Matthew 7:24-27 (NKJV):

(Build on the Rock)

[24]*"Therefore whoever hears these sayings of Mine, and does them, I will liken him to a wise man who built his house on the rock: [25] and the rain descended, the floods came, and the winds blew and beat on that house; and it did not fall, for it was founded on the rock. [26]"But everyone who hears these sayings of Mine, and does not do them, will be like a foolish man who built his house on the sand: [27] and the rain descended, the floods came, and the winds blew and beat on that house; and it fell. And great was its fall."*

Your righteousness is not the Rock that Mathew 7 is referring to, when your righteousness is not of Christ.

Deuteronomy 6:25 (NKJV):

(Your Righteousness)

Then it will be righteousness for us, if we are careful to observe all these commandments before the Lord our God, as He has commanded us.

Romans 10:3-4 (NKJV):

(Christ's Righteousness from God)

"*3For they being ignorant of God's righteousness, and seeking to establish their own righteousness, have not submitted to the righteousness of God. 4For Christ is the end of the law for righteousness to everyone who believes.*"

However, Jesus came to change that perception in Deut. 6:25. We no longer need the law as a school master forcing pupils to obey, because Jesus is the answer to being right with God. However, there are some who still feel the law is their school master and will not deviate from what they believe. Some don't do it for wrong reasons intentionally but out of ignorance. There was a time when I also did things out of ignorance.

When our service to God is based on man's tradition, we are not working for God neither would we receive the house that God built. Hence, we do not receive the blessings from the work that Christ has done for us, to be right with God.

Man gets you embroiled in traditions and work, taking you away from Christ, and thereby causing you to fall into sin. The Pharisees had this point of view, and they were right, through the laws that God gave Moses for them. However, doing it that way, do not give you the justification Christ guaranteed for you by faith, After the Cross.

Galatians 3:23-25 (NKJV):

"*23 But before faith came, we were kept under guard by the law, kept for the faith which would afterward be revealed.*

24 Therefore the law was our tutor to bring us to Christ, that we might be justified by faith.

25 But after faith has come, we are no longer under a tutor."

Christianity has declined greatly since the early 1900s in the United States. There have been many reasons attributed to why America has experienced such a decrease in Christianity. Some of which are:

1. Lack of interest.

2. The feeling that it is not important to go to Church anymore.

3. Gradual phasing out of people's belief.

4. A change in the method of worship.

These are all genuine reasons from people, but have we really studied the teachings of the churches? Christ says, *"If I am lifted up from the earth, I will draw all peoples to Myself"*

Has the Church been lifting up Jesus? Have we been lifting up the law? We should remember Paul's caution that if anyone preaches any other gospel besides the one he preaches, let them be accursed (Galatians 1:6-9 niv, nlt).

GALATIANS 1:6-9 (NIV)
(Who has pulled you from the Grace)

6 I am astonished that you are so quickly deserting the one who called you to live in the grace of Christ and are turning to a different gospel—

7 which is really no gospel at all. Evidently some people are throwing you into confusion and are trying to pervert the gospel of Christ.

8 But even if we or an angel from heaven should preach a gospel other than the one we preached to you, let them be under God's curse!

9 As we have already said, so now I say again: If anybody is preaching to you a gospel other than what you accepted, let them be under God's curse!

THE SAME GOSPEL FROM THE BIBLE CAN AND WILL BRING YOU CURSES OR GRACE BOTH GOSPEL'S COME FROM THE BIBLE, ITS THE SAME BIBLE, THAT'S PUTTING YOU UNDER CURSES OR GRACE. HOWEVER, THE GOSPEL MUST BE RIGHTFULLY DIVIDED TO RECEIVE GRACE FROM READING AND TEACHING IT!!

Do the Church know what Gospel Paul preached?

Have the Church strayed from that teaching of GRACE?

Have they been using the laws to keep them from sinning, as a way to be right with God?

And if they have been using the law to make people right with God, they do not understand they have been placing themselves and the people they teach back up under the Curses Christ delivered them from caused by the Law! Because using the Law wrongfully puts them back under the Curses (Galatians 5:4 Amp) Christ removed from their lives (Galatian 3:13 Amp).

GALATIANS 3:13 Amp

(Christ redeemed us from the Curse of the Law)

13 Christ purchased our freedom and redeemed us from the curse of the Law and its condemnation by becoming a curse for us—for it is written, "CURSED IS EVERYONE WHO HANGS [crucified] ON A TREE (cross)"—

GALATIANS 5:3-4 NLT

(TRYING to be JUSTIFIED by the law WE Distant our self from Christ and Fall from GRACE)

3 I'll say it again. If you are trying to find favor with God by being circumcised, you must obey every regulation in the whole law of Moses.

4 For if you are TRYING to MAKE YOURSELVES RIGHT with GOD by keeping the law, you have been cut off from CHRIST! You have FALLEN FROM AWAY from GOD'S 's GRACE.

~IF KEEPING THE LAW DOESN'T MAKE US RIGHT OR JUSTIFY US WITH GOD? ~

~HOW CAN WE BE MADE RIGHT AND JUSTIFIED WITH GOD BY GOD'S STANDARDS? ~

GALATIANS 5: 5-6 NLT
(God's way of making you right with himself "After The Cross" is Through Christ)

5 But we who live by the Spirit eagerly wait to receive by FAITH the RIGHTEOUSNESS GOD HAS PROMISED to US. For when we place our faith in CHRIST JESUS, there is no benefit in being circumcised or being uncircumcised. What is important is FAITH EXPRESSING ITSELF in LOVE.

"[AND YOU MUST NOT BE AFRAID TO TEACH GRACE THAT IS THE GOSPEL THAT CHRIST GAVE PAUL TO PREACHED]

GALATIANS 1:10 niv"

10 Am I now trying to win the approval of human beings, or of God? Or am I trying to please people? If I were still trying to please people, I would not be a servant of Christ.

Galatians 3:10-11; NKJV:

(Cursed is anyone continuing in the law)

"[10] For as many as are of the works of the law are under the curse; for it is written, "Cursed is everyone who does not continue in all things which are written in the book of the law, to do them." [11] But that no one is justified by the law in the sight of God is evident, for "the just shall live by faith"

Have they been preaching any other gospel other than what Paul preached? If so, is the Gospel they preach accursed? Which, in turn, will cause the people to be cursed? When we take all of that in consideration, we can see why there is a possible decline in Church attendance. They are not preaching the Gospel that Paul preached, hence putting themselves and everyone else they are teaching in bondage of the Curse.

God says the Scriptures was given for *reproof, correction, and for instruction in righteousness (1 Timothy 3:16- 17)* and *not instructions in the law*

Paul would have to enjoin us to present every *man* as perfect in Christ Jesus. To do this, we have to show them they are right with God through the sacrifice Christ has made for them, which makes them right with God. They have to accept the righteousness of God through faith in what Christ has done for them and not their own righteousness through the law (Deut. 6:25). There is a big difference. There is a different righteousness that does not come through the Righteousness of Christ after the Cross (Romans 10:3-4).

Chapter 2
Are We Separating God's Kingdom?

Do not separate God's kingdom by fighting each other over your differences. Your own desires and pride could be causing you to fight; pride is an abomination to God. also, sowing discord among the brethren is something God hates as an abomination!

Proverbs 6:16-19 (NKJV):

These six things the Lord hates, Yes, seven are an abomination to Him: A Proud Look, A lying tongue, Hands that shed innocent blood, A heart that devises wicked plans, Feet that are swift in running to evil, A false witness who speaks lies, And one who sows discord among brethren.

Under this section, we see how hatred leads us away from God's love. We learn the value of loving one another, forgiving one another, and supporting one another in Christ. We also learn the immense importance of solving our conflicts before they get the better of us. I gave this particular topic a special attention due to the current level of hatred among people—a lot of which are perpetrated in social media and other media forms.

If you watch around you, you will notice that people talk with a lot of spite against each other. They do not care about each other even in their business dealings. Their greatest concern is for them to gain something of value regardless how many people they hurt to get it.

But how do you learn to love people who are so spiteful and those who don't care about you? Following the readings shared in this book is the way. It considers the fact that people will try to agitate you even when you try to love them. Before you start reading this section of the book, please note the following questions and answer them personally:

1. What's the worst thing that a person ever did to you?
2. Are there things you feel that you can never forgive? Why so?
3. Why do you think Christians fight with each other over religion and how they choose to serve God, be it the seeker-sensitive gospel, prosperity gospel, what day they serve, the Sabbath?

As you read through this section, you will realize that Jesus came on earth to set us free and show us that all sins can be forgiven. If God Himself can forgive us for the most grievous sins, how much more us, shouldn't we forgive each other? While reading, be intentional to learn something about forgiveness and loving one another.

2 Timothy 2:14 (NLT):

*Remind everyone about these things, and command them in God's presence to **stop fighting over words**. Such arguments are useless, and they can ruin those who hear them.*

Romans 14:1-4 (NLT):

(Do not fight over differences)

Accept other believers who are weak in faith, and don't argue with them about what they think is right or wrong.

For instance, one person believes it's all right to eat anything. But another believer with a sensitive conscience will eat only vegetables. Those who feel free to eat anything must not look down on those who don't. Similarly, those who don't eat certain foods mustn't condemn those who do, for God has accepted them. Who are you to condemn someone else's servants? Their own master will judge whether they stand or fall. And with the Lord's help, they will stand and receive his approval.

GOD did not bring us together through His Righteousness to fight each other. He would rather we humble ourselves and back out. He doesn't need us to fight for Him. He needs us to humble ourselves and let Him use us to win souls.

God lets you know that you are fighting because of your own desires and not His (James 4:1-2). His word, also, states that people who want to fight and cause division are to be avoided because they do not serve Jesus (Romans 16-18).

This reminds me of a true story that happened on my job. I was protecting a young guy from this other religion's teachings of false doctrines (so I thought). I kept pointing out the lies this other guy was trying to teach the young guy. I kept showing him in the Bible the lies he was trying to get him to believe, and it got a little heated between him and me, so I left the area. Now, when I got outside, the Holy Spirit spoke to me and said, "I don't need you to fight for me, I want his soul too." My whole perception of fighting for Christ changed that moment.

The next few scriptures will give you the basics of how Christ would like us to handle such situations as I experienced above.

1 Timothy 6:20-21 (NKJV):

(Guard the Faith)

²⁰ O Timothy! Guard what was committed to your trust, avoiding the profane and idle babblings and contradictions of what is falsely called knowledge— ²¹ by professing it some have strayed concerning the faith. Grace be with you. Amen.

James 4:1-2 (NKJV):

(Pride promotes strife, and not righteousness.)

Where do wars and fights come from among you? Do they not come from your desires for pleasure that war in your members? You lust and do not have. You murder and covet and cannot obtain. You fight and war. Yet; you do not have because you do not ask.

Romans 16:17-18 (NKJV):

(Avoid those who cause division, they serve their own belly) Now I urge you, brethren, note those who cause divisions and offenses, contrary to the doctrine which you learned, and avoid them. For those who are such do not serve our Lord Jesus Christ, but their own belly, and by smooth words and flattering speech deceive the hearts of the simple.

Some people read this next verse and think they are supposed to go out and fight for Jesus. Jesus stated that He could call down twelve legions of angels to fight for Him (Matt. 26:53), but His calling to save was bigger than His desire to save Himself. Jesus did not serve His own desires. James 4:1-2 would then tell us that "the reason we fight is because of our own desires." So, you out there discussing or planning about fighting for Jesus, note that the Bible says you are fighting for your own desires.

Matthew 26:52-54 (NKJV):

(Take sword Parish by sword)

[52] But Jesus said to him, "Put your sword in its place, for all who take the sword will perish by the sword. [53] Or do you think that I cannot now pray to My Father, and He will provide Me with more than twelve legions of angels? [54] How then could the Scriptures be fulfilled, that it must happen thus?"

The Bible says we should put our swords in its place. We know the Bible references the sword as the Word of God too (**Eph. 6:17, Heb. 4:12; NKJV**). So, put your words back in your mouth. Yet, you want to use God's Word to war with someone else because you think you're right or in other words, because of your desires.

Ephesians 6:17 (NKJV):

And take the helmet of salvation, and the sword of the Spirit, which is the word of God;

Exodus 15:3:

The Lord is a man of war; The Lord is His name.

(God is the warrior, not you. God will do the fighting for you) (Exodus 14:14 and Revelation 19:11).

You must understand that in the spiritual, God fights for you. Hence, your agitation to fight is for your own desires.

34

Exodus 14:13-14 (NKJV):

And Moses said to the people, "Do not be afraid. Stand still, and see the salvation of the Lord, which He will accomplish for you today. For the Egyptians whom you see today, you shall see again no more forever. The Lord will fight for you, and you shall Hold Your Peace."

God will also fight with you and besides you so that you will get the victory.

1 Samuel 14:10 (NKJV):

But if they say thus, 'Come up to us,' then we will go up. For the Lord has delivered them into our hand, and this will be a sign to us."

1 Timothy 6:4-5 (NKJV):

He is proud, knowing nothing, but is obsessed with disputes and arguments over words, from which come envy, strife, reviling, evil suspicions, useless wrangling's of men of corrupt minds and destitute of the truth, who suppose that godliness is a means of gain. From such withdraw yourself.

1 Timothy 6:20-21 (NKJV):

O Timothy! Guard what was committed to your trust, avoiding the profane and idle babblings and contradictions of what is falsely called knowledge—by professing it some have strayed concerning the faith. Grace be with you. Amen.

1 Timothy 1:5-8 (NKJV):

(Strayed from the truth, becoming teachers of the law)

Now the purpose of the commandment is love from a pure heart, from a good conscience, and from sincere faith, from which some, having strayed, have turned aside to idle talk, desiring to be teachers of the law, understanding neither what they say nor the things which they affirm.

Rev. 19:11

"Now I saw heaven opened, and behold, a white horse. And He who sat on him was called Faithful and True, and in righteousness He judges and makes war."

If God is going to make war, we don't have to, because the battle is not ours, but His (2 Chronicles 20:15). Besides, God gives an inheritance to those who don't return evil for evil (1 Peter 3:9-10). Fighting with each other is not what God has called us to do. Jesus did not do that when He was being crucified on the cross. He responded with a blessing on them: "Father, forgive them, for they do not know what they do. (Luke 23:34)

1 Peter 3:9-10 (NKJV):

(You inherit a Blessing when you do not return evil for evil)

⁹ *Not returning evil for evil or reviling for reviling, but on the Contrary Blessing, knowing that you were called to this, that you may inherit a blessing.* ¹⁰ *For "He who would love life and see good days, let him refrain his tongue from evil, and his lips from speaking deceit.*

Offended or offensive?

The devil is trying to separate our communities using either of the above: the one who was offended or the one who offended. This is a spiritual attack on the unity of Christ. And "I see this devil's spiritual attack targeted specifically on the unity of Christ's followers."

Proverbs 19:11; NKJV:

"The discretion of a man makes him slow to anger, and his glory is to overlook a transgression."

1 Corinthians 13:7:

"Bears all things, believes all things, hopes all things, endures all things."

This is where we should begin with interpersonal conflicts resolution between fellow believers. We should first try to overlook an offense and love one another in such a way as to believe the best about our brother or sister-in-Christ, by assuming initially that any offense was unintentional.

Mathew 5:21-25; NKJV:

You have heard that it was said to those of old, 'You shall not murder, and whoever murders will be in danger of the judgment.' But I say to you that whoever is angry with his brother without a cause shall be in danger of the judgment. And whoever says to his brother, 'Raca!' shall be in danger of the council. But whoever says, 'You fool!' shall be in danger of hell fire. Therefore if you bring your gift to the altar, and there remember that your brother has something against you, leave your gift there before the altar, and go your way. First be reconciled to your brother, and then come and offer your gift. Agree with your adversary quickly, while you are on the way with him, lest your adversary deliver you to the judge, the judge hand you over to the officer and you be thrown into prison.

When you have offered up your apology by order of the scriptures, I have to be obedient and accept. I am nobody in the bigger picture of Christ. Who would I be to turn my back on a brother or sister-in-Christ?

The reason I wrote this section, is in the hopes that when others read this, they will be gentle and kind with their words. I have seen a lot of hateful words in the Christ-following community in social media and other forums, and it hurts my heart. More so, it is established that when change occurs, whether in a church setting, at work, or home, stress levels can rise and emotions can be affected.

Sometimes, even though we are brothers and sisters-in-Christ, we can become offended, hurt, or be angry with one another. Some of the times, these offenses are totally unintended and often, the person who causes the offense is not even aware that it has taken place. But when these do happen, we should be guided by how the Scriptures instructed us to respond.

Love and let's Forgive our Brothers and Sisters by Living in Love

Out of love, God offered His only Son to die on the cross to save us from sin. We were bound by law, but after Jesus' death on the cross, we were set free. This is the kind of love this book encourages us to profess. It points out some obvious mistakes we make when dealing with our brothers and sisters-in-Christ. It gives us guidance on what to do when a conflict arises between our fellow Christians or any other people around and us.

We are obliged to accept apologies when they are sincerely offered and also forgive those who wrong us just like we would like to be forgiven ourselves when we are in the wrong. Christ is love, and all those who are called by His name must love too. He instructed us to love and forgive our enemies, for our fight with the enemy is spiritual and not physical. Some may agree with aggressiveness, while others may not. That in itself is separation.

However, the Bible teaches us to approach our opponents with gentleness so that God himself can win them from the snares of the devil (**2 Timothy 2:25-26**).

If we use our words kindly, God will handle the situation and we as Christ's followers will get the victory and God will get the glory! And we stay unified as we defeat the devil's trick to separate!

Romans 12:4-5:

For as we have many members in one body and all the members do not have the same function, so we, being many, are one body in Christ, and individually members of one of another.

The devil is trying to use our *individuality* to separate us in Christ ... when Christ has clearly put us together...!!!

Yes, my Brothers and Sisters-in-Christ, we have the same blood running through our veins—that is, Jesus. The devil knows your will is strong and progressive. He knows God has you on a new assignment and every assignment God placed you on, you were able to surmount it. However, this is your hardest assignment because it causes you to stand down when your spirit says fight. Remember, Jesus said in Mathew 26:53 that He could ask the Father for 12 legions of angels to fight His battle, but that was not His assignment, so He did not but He humbled Himself for a greater cause, and that was for our Salvation.

The righteousness of Christ is what he has done for us; He has given us His righteousness so we can be obedient to the call of God in our lives.

The level God is about to take you to requires a different you. Obedience, especially when you are in the right, is the hardest thing for a Christian to accomplish. As I teach the Christians, God has put under me, *the lessons in obedience*, one of the progressive truths is this: being obedient for the greater good, even when you're right about a situation, is the hardest thing to do. However, that brings elevation in your trials from God Himself.

LUKE 2:48-52 talks about how God elevated Jesus in Stature, Wisdom, and Favor with men and God.

While I was at work, a guy I worked with was very vulgar and used to curse around me all the time. I would keep reading my Bible and talking to people about Christ. One day, just the two of us were in the break room. He was going through some great hardship. He came to me and said, "Excuse me, I always see you reading your Bible on break and in the locker rooms, talking about God, could you pray for me?" Wow! God gave me the opportunity to drop a seed of salvation into his spirit and soul while I prayed for him.

The greater good was his soul, not him cursing and hurting my spirit. Jesus did not call His legions of angels to defend Him when they spit, beat, and cursed Him out, to destroy His character. He was thinking about us, and about connecting us back to His Father. Jesus took all that abuse for us, so it was not much for me to take a little cursing.

TO EVERYONE WHO READS THIS NEXT PAGE

The reason God has called you to this new realm of obedience is because your assignment has changed. You will unify a nation through the Spirit of God who will use you. You will pass the trials you are about to face, and God will increase you with Wisdom, Stature, and Favor with God and man through your Obedience to humble yourself. God wants to fight all your battles so that God gets the Glory for winning them.

Again, I leave you with a scripture from the Lord.

Remember when Jesus' mother was looking for Him and she found Him in the temple? Jesus said to her: "Didn't you know I would be about my Father's business?" (Luke 2: 48-52). In the next verse, He submitted to her and followed them. Right after that submissive and obedient move, the

Bible says Jesus increased in "wisdom, stature, and in favor with God and men" (Luke 2: 52).

He was doing His Father's business; however, His increase in wisdom, stature, and favor with God and men was bestowed only after He was obedient and submissive to His parents. Then God gave Him the increase in all those things. God is changing you for the mission He has for you. He is going to give you all those gifts He gave Jesus, but it will only come from your obedience to a humbling Spirit.

Luke 2:48-52 (NKJV)

48 So when they saw Him, they were amazed; and His mother said to Him, "Son, why have You done this to us? Look, your father and I have sought you anxiously."

49 And He said to them, "Why did you seek me? Did you not know that I must be about My Father's business?"

50 But they did not understand the statement which He spoke to them.

Jesus Advances in Wisdom and Favor

51 Then He went down with them and came to Nazareth, and was subject to them, but His mother kept all these things in her heart.

52 And Jesus increased in wisdom and stature, and in favor with God and men.

 I love you my Brothers AND Sisters; God has emptied me; receive the anointing and move towards your higher calling.

I see the spiritual warfare. I know there is a calling on your life to free some of God's people. However, He is giving you a new heart and mind for this mission. God has called me to free the mind of His people in the spiritual realm. I see the anointing on the lives of God's people, and that's why the tests are going to be strong. However, God Himself is going to have you handle things differently if you allow Him to.

We all need God; this battle for souls is His, not ours to fight. He will fight it for us, so we can go pick up the spoils. You will do great work for God when He gives you a new heart; it will also come with a new mission for the souls God will use you to draw to His Kingdom.

We are all united in a battle for souls God has given (2 Chronicles 20:15) you and me. This battle is bigger than us, and we cannot fight it alone (1 Samuel 14:10). "For the battle is not ours; it is the Lord's." My spirit is showing me this scripture is for all of us, my brothers and Sisters-in-Christ.

2 Chronicles 20:15 (NIV)

He said: "Listen, King Jehoshaphat and all who live in Judah and Jerusalem! (Your circle of friends) This is what the LORD says to you: 'Do not be afraid or discouraged because of this vast army. For the battle is not yours, but God's."

For His miraculous power to be manifested on our behavior, we have to draw His people together on one accord to first pray and praise Him. We will fight in the spiritual realm through prayer; then God will fight for us (2 Chronicle 20:15) in the spiritual and carnal realm as He did with King Jehoshaphat. Then we can walk in together and pick up all the spoils that are left from God's victory over the evil one. In other words, we will pick up the souls for God together. He will get all the Glory, and we'll get the Victory!

P.S. The new heart God is giving us all will draw a new group of people to His Kingdom—some of the people you already know and some you don't know. God will use you to remove their stony hearts.

God already knew these things that are happening now would happen. E.g. churches coming against true biblical beliefs in the way they serve and are removing Christ's followers biblical beliefs from our country. In the spiritual realm, God showed me that the devil's trick is to get us to focus on things that will not draw souls to Christ before God comes back. That is, being evangelizers in our own country and abroad. I'll leave you with the two scriptures that I will obey and keep until God calls us home.

2 Timothy 2:25-26 (NIV)

[25]*Opponents must be gently instructed, in the hope that God will grant them repentance leading them to a knowledge of the truth,* [26]*and that they will come to their senses and escape from the trap of the devil, who has taken them captive to do his will.*

2 Timothy 4:3-5 (NIV)

[3]*"For the time will come when people will not put up with sound doctrine. Instead, to suit their own desires, they will gather around them a great number of teachers to say what their itching ears want to hear.* [4] *They will turn their ears away from the truth and turn aside to myths.* [5] *But you, keep your head in all situations, endure hardship,*

Do the work of an evangelist, fulfill all the duties of your ministry.

I love you all and my prayers are with you openly and behind your back as well. God said, "Evangelize, stay true to the ministry I gave you."

I want to respond to that verse. From my understanding, what I believe God is saying in this verse is this: people are going to raise up false teachers for themselves and are not going to honor His Word.

You see, God is telling us He already knows these things are going to happen. How do we know this? He wrote this verse over two thousand years ago before we were born. He also wrote in His Word what to do when this happens.

2 Timothy 4:5 (NKJV)

But you be watchful in all things, endure afflictions, do the work of an evangelist, fulfill your ministry.

He implore us to endure afflictions (people talking about us, betraying or persecuting us). Still, He wants us to be evangelists (a person who seeks to draw others to the conversion of followers to Christ by faith for their salvation) and fulfill our ministry. And our ministry is drawing people to Christ for salvation. If our ministry is to follow Christ, we must understand what He CAME for...

John 3:17

"For God sent not his Son into the world not to condemn the world; but that the world through him might be saved."

John 12:47

"And if any man hears my words, and believe not, I judge him not: for I came not to judge the world, but to save the world.

From my understanding of God's word (2 Timothy 4:35), do not get tricked by these false teachers and DO NOT forget fighting amongst each other does not promote the KINGDOM of GOD. We must understand that our PRIDE is something that causes fights from our own desires to be right or prove that we were right. This is not the Righteousness of God.

See, God will rebuke Satan for you, and this is His way of showing that He loves you and you don't have to fight because you don't belong to Satan anymore (Zech. 3:2; NKJV).

Zechariah 3:2 (NKJV)

2 And the Lord said to Satan, "The Lord rebuke you, Satan! The Lord who has chosen Jerusalem rebuke you! Is this not a brand plucked from the fire?"

James 4:1-2 (NKJV)

(Pride Promotes Strife, and not Righteousness.)

1 Where do wars and fights come from among you? Do they not come from your desires for pleasure that war in your members?

2 You lust and do not have. You murder and covet and cannot obtain.

You fight and war. Yet; you do not have because you do not ask.

The Bible teaches us to approach our opponents with gentleness, not fight to prove we are right. God wants to win them over, and He can't do His job if you are trying to do it for Him.

2 Timothy 2:25-26 (NIV)

25Opponents must be gently instructed, in the hope that God will grant them repentance leading them to a knowledge of the truth, 26 and that they will come to their senses and escape from the trap of the devil, who has taken them captive to do his will.

Chapter 3
Are You Working for God in Vain?

Mark 10:30

(Bless hundred-fold on earth and eternal life in heaven)

Are you working TO or FROM something!!?

Are you working to be right with God? Or are you working from the position of knowing you're right with God because of what Christ did on the Cross?

2 Timothy 4:3-5

(Not enduring sound doctrine. Evangelize and stay true to the Ministry I gave you)

Psalms 127:1

(Unless God builds the house)

Unless the Lord builds the house, they labor in vain who build it; unless the Lord guards the city, the watchman stays awake in vain.

Isaiah 64:6

(Your right living is as filthy rags)

I Corinthians 3:11-15 (NKJV)
(Your work will be a loss, you will be saved though)

For No other Foundation can anyone lay than that which is Laid, which is Jesus Christ. Now if anyone builds on this foundation with gold, silver, precious stones, wood, hay, straw, each one's work will become clear; for the Day will declare it, because it will be revealed by fire; and the fire will test each one's work, of what sort it is. If anyone's work which he has built on it endures, he will receive a reward." (Vs.15): "If anyone's work is burned, he will suffer loss; but he himself will be saved, yet so as through fire."

This section mainly describes working for God, explaining the difference between actually serving God and working in vain. It is vital because it could save us the agony of having to suffer in hell when we thought we were fully committed to serving God. Unless we allow ourselves to be used by God to fulfill His mission, then all we do, we do it in vain. When we surrender our lives to God and offer our hearts as a sacrifice to God, God dwells in us and uses us to fulfill His purpose. Unless you are building on the foundation God has built which is Christ (1 Corinthians 3:11; NKJV), you are working in vain (Psalms 127:1; NKJV). As you read through this section, meditate about the following questions:

1. Have you ever done some work, only to realize that all you did was useless? How did that make you feel?

2. Would you continue working if you found out that whatever you were working on wouldn't bear any fruits in the end?

3. How many times have you followed your heart's desires while ignoring God's will for you?

Under this section, you get to know whether the kind of life you are currently leading will be rewarded or if it is in vain. If you do it to look good or to try and be right with God, then you are doing it in vain. Christ made you right with God "After the Cross" (Romans 10:3-4; NKJV) (Philippians 3:8-9; NKJV).

2 Chronicles 20:15 (NKJV)

(Battles is not yours)

And he said, "Listen, all you of Judah and you inhabitants of Jerusalem, and you, King Jehoshaphat! Thus says the Lord to you: 'Do not be afraid nor dismay because of this great multitude, for the battle is not yours, but God's.

Ezekiel 36:22 (NKJV)

(God Does It For Himself! Not You!)

"Therefore say to the house of Israel, 'Thus says the Lord God: "I do not do this for your sake, O house of Israel, but for My holy name's sake, which you have profaned among the nations wherever you went.

Ezekiel 36:24-30 (NKJV)

(God is Rebuilding and Cleansing You)

[24]For I will take you from among the nations, gather you out of all countries, and bring you into your own land. Then I will sprinkle clean water on you, and you shall be clean; I will cleanse you from all your filthiness and from all your idols. I will give you a new heart and put a new spirit within you;

Galatians 3:14 (NKJV)

"That the blessing of Abraham might come upon the Gentiles in Christ Jesus, that we might receive the promise of the Spirit through faith".)

Ezekiel 36:26-30 (NKJV)

*I will take the heart of stone out of your flesh and give you a heart of flesh. I will put My Spirit within you (**read Galatians 1: 15-16 The Spirit God put in you is what Paul reveals is Christ in You**) and cause you to walk in My statutes, and you will keep My judgments and do them. Then you shall dwell in the land that I gave to your fathers; you shall be My people, and I will be your God. I will deliver you from all your uncleanness. I will call for the grain and multiply it, and bring no famine upon you. And I will multiply the fruit of your trees and the increase of your fields, so that you need never again bear the reproach of famine among the nations."*

Ezekiel 36:31-32

*(**First, He blesses you, then you feel bad about your sins**) Then you will re-member your evil ways and your deeds that were not good; and you will loathe yourselves in your own sight, for your iniquities and your abominations. Not for your sake do I do this," says the Lord God "let it be known to you. Be ashamed and confounded for your own ways, O house of Israel!"*

You see, God Himself does everything for His Glory; He even sanctify His name through you in Ezekiel 36: 23. All these blessings come from Ezekiel 36:22-32 and Galatians 3:14, 2 Chronicles 20:15,

- ✦ He pulls you out of your mess
- ✦ He cleanses you by sprinkling clean water on you.
- ✦ He cleanses you from all your filthiness and idols

- He gives you a new heart

- He puts a new spirit in you.

- Christ ties us to the Blessings of Abraham

- He removes your Heart of Stone

- He causes you to walk in His statutes

- He will deliver you from all your uncleanness

- I will never let you bear famine again.

- HOW do I receive the Covenant Promise?

Hebrews 8: 6-13 (NKJV)

(Christ put us in a New Covenant)

But now He has obtained a more excellent ministry, inasmuch as He is also Mediator of a better covenant, which was established on better promises.

Hebrews 8:7-9; (NKJV)

7For if that first covenant had been faultless, then no place would have been sought for a second. 8 Because finding fault with them, He says "Behold, the days are coming, says the Lord, when I will make a new covenant with the house of Israel and with the house of Judah— 9 not according to the covenant that I made with their fathers in the day when I took them by the hand to lead them out of the land of Egypt; because they did not continue in My covenant, and I disregarded them, says the Lord. (Heb. 8:10): For this is the covenant that I will make with the house of Israel after those days, says the Lord: I will put My laws in their mind and write them on their hearts; and I will be their God, and they shall be My people.

(Ezekiel 36:28 says same)

None of them shall teach his neighbor, and none his brother, saying, 'Know the Lord,' for all shall know Me, from the least of them to the greatest of them. For I will be merciful to their unrighteousness, and their sins and their lawless deeds I will remember no more." In that He says, "A new covenant," He has made the first obsolete. Now what is becoming obsolete and growing old is ready to vanish away (Hebrews 8:11-13).

Hebrews 9:14-15 (NKJV)

(Christ New Covenant blood)

*How much more shall the blood of **Christ**, who through the eternal Spirit offered Himself without spot to God, cleanse your conscience from (Dead Works) to serve the living God? And for this reason, He is the Mediator of the new covenant, by means of death, for the redemption of the transgressions under the first covenant, that those who are called may receive the promise of the (eternal inheritance.)*

John 6:63 (NLT)

Spirit alone gives eternal life, human effort accomplishes nothing.

Galatians 3:8-9

(Justified and blessed)

Are you using the law to be right and justified with god? Or are you working in vain?

Galatian 3: 10-11 (NKJV):

No one is justified by the law, you are under a curse.

Galatian 3:13, Numbers 23:8 (NKJV)

Christ redeemed us from the curse of the law

Numbers 23:8 (NKJV)

Who can curse whom God has blessed

Are you working to be blessed by god, or are you working in vain?

How do we know we are up under the Covenant Blessings of God?

Galatians 3:14-17 (NKJV)

(Jesus ties us to the Blessing of Abraham)

14 that the blessing of Abraham might come upon the Gentiles in Christ Jesus, that we might receive the promise of the Spirit through faith.

(The Changeless Promise)

15 Brethren, I speak in the manner of men: Though it is only a man's covenant, yet if it is confirmed, no one annuls or adds to it. 16 Now to Abraham and his Seed were the promises made. He does not say, "And to seeds," as of many, but as of one, "And to your Seed," who is Christ. 17 And this I say, that the law, which was four hundred and thirty years later, cannot annul the covenant that was confirmed before by God in Christ, that it should make the promise of no effect.

So, even today, we are still entitled to the blessings of Abraham because God made this Covenant, so it cannot be annulled. These blessings can only accessed by faith in Christ. So, if you are trying to work to receive these by keeping laws? You Are Working In Vain!

How do we know that we are entitled to the Blessings of Abraham without works? Galatians 3 talks about one, the Blesser, CHRIST JESUS, who tied us to the spirit and blessings of Abraham by making us Sons and Daughters of Abraham spiritually by Faith.)

Galatians 3:29 (NKJV)

²⁹*And if you are Christ's, then you are Abraham's seed, and heirs according to the promise.*

See, we already have the entitlement to the covenant blessings that God made with Abraham. Not because we have worked to deserve it. The truth is, Christ is the reason it belongs to us if we have faith in the redemptive work He did **After the Cross** <u>*for us*</u>.

Luke 11:13

(Evil one gives good gifts, how much more will God give the Holy Spirit)

What Are some of the Blessings of Abraham?

Gen 12:2-3 (NKJV)

(Blessing of Abraham)

I will make you a great nation; I will bless you and make your name great; and you shall be a blessing. I will bless those who bless you, And I will curse him who curses you; and in you all the families of the earth shall be BLESSED."

ARE WE RIGHTFULLY JUDGING OTHERS, OR ARE WE JUDGING IN VAIN?

John 12:47 (NKJV)

(I did not come to judge but to save)

Mathew 6:33 (NKJV)

[33] *But seek first the kingdom of God and His righteousness, and all these things shall be added to you.* [34] *Therefore do not worry about tomorrow, for tomorrow will worry about its own things. Sufficient for the day is its own trouble.*

Philippians 3:3-9 (NKJV)

(Paul says he gives it all up to gain what Christ did for him)

For we are the circumcision, who worship God in the Spirit, rejoice in Christ Jesus, and have no confidence in the flesh, though I also might have confidence in the flesh. If anyone else thinks he may have confidence in the flesh, I more so: circumcised the eighth day, of the stock of Israel, of the tribe of Benjamin, a Hebrew of the Hebrews; concerning the law, a Pharisee; concerning zeal, persecuting the church; concerning the righteousness which is in the law, blameless. But what things were gain to me, these I have counted loss for Christ. (8) Yet indeed I also count all things loss for the excellence of the knowledge of "Christ Jesus my Lord, for whom I have suffered the loss of all things, and count them as rubbish, that I MAY GAIN CHRIST (9) and be found in Him, Not Having My Own RIGHTEOUSNESS, which is FROM the LAW, but that which is through **Faith in Christ, the Righteousness which is from God by faith;**

Are you working to be right by the law with

God, or are you working in vain?

ROMANS 10:3-4 (NKJV) *(Have not accepted my Righteousness, Establishing their own Righteousness)*

ROMANS 8:3-4 (NKJV)

"Christ fulfills the Law for You!"

After completing this section, you should be able to identify things that you are obliged to do by your own initiative and those which you should allow God to use you to do them. For instance, God does not want us to argue with nonbelievers on things concerning the faith. He wants us to only guide them where we can. He also keeps His promises and blesses us abundantly if we follow Christ and have faith in what He has done for us **"After the Cross,"** like Christ making us right with God (1 Cor. 1:30) (Philippians 3:9).

There is a different righteousness, one different from your own (Deut. 6:25; NKJV). This is the righteousness you see in Mathew 6:33 called "His Righteousness." God let us know that there is a different righteousness when He says in Romans 10:3 (NKJV), "For they being ignorant of God's righteousness, and seeking to establish their own righteousness, have not submitted to the righteousness of God." We must operate in the right Righteousness of God; otherwise, we will be "Working in Vain" because this has already been established for us in Christ. Paul clears all this up in a nice profound statement. He says in Philippians 3:9, "And be found in Him, not having my own righteousness, which *is* from the law, but that which *is* through faith in Christ, the righteousness which is from God by faith."

Romans 3:22-26 (NLT)

(Christ makes us Right with God)

²² *We are made right with God by placing our faith in Jesus Christ.*

And this is true for everyone who believes, no matter who we are.

Romans 5:1-2 (NLT)

(Right with God through Christ)

1Therefore, since we have been made right in God's sight by faith, we have peace with God Because of what Jesus Christ our Lord has done for us. 2Because of our faith, Christ has brought us into this place of undeserved privilege where we now stand, and we confidently and joyfully look forward to sharing God's glory.

- So, **are** you are working to receive the blessing of God? (**Galatian 3:14-17, 29; NKJV**)

- **Do** you go out judging people and their lifestyle for Christ? (**John 12:47; NKJV**)

- **Are** you trying to be right with God through the law? (**Romans 10:4; NKJV**)

- **Are** you trying to change yourself to be right with God? (**Ezekiel 36:26-40**)

- **Are** you trying to be justified by the law? (**Galatian 3:1011**)

- **Are** you doing it for yourself because you think that's what God wants? (**Ezekiel 36:22; NKJV**)

- **Do** you believe you must fight battles to be useful to God? (**2 Chronicles 20:15**)

- **Are** you trying to receive the Righteousness of God by the Law? (**Romans 10:4**)

If you believe you have to keep all the laws (commandments) to have eternal life (john 6:63; NLT), "then, you are working in vain!"

Chapter 4
What is FROM GLORY to GLORY?

Leaving the law and going into the Righteousness of God.

2 Corinthians 3:7-18 (NKJV)

(Glory of the New Covenant)

From Glory to Glory

In this section, I will clarify what is meant by "the law." You might get confused when I ask you to obey God's command and at the same time, inform you that you are no longer under the law. So, what does it mean not to be under the law and to be obedient to God's commandments? We are required to exercise our freedom from the law with a lot of responsibility. We are obliged to live well with each other, in accordance with God's commandments which were summarized to one law of love. Jesus did not come to destroy the law but rather, to fulfill it.

Through His death, we were elevated from glory to glory. When we were under the law, our righteousness was judged by the law. Now that we are no longer under the law, the blood of Jesus has cleansed us and paid for all our sins. **We are made Righteous through Faith in what** Jesus did for us **(1 Cor. 1:30; NKJV) "After the Cross."** In essence, we moved from a point where we were judged strictly by law to a point where we are treated with love and God's mercy through Christ **(1 Peter 1:3)**. Initially, we were made right with God through the Old Covenant, which was made between God and the Israelites at Mt. Sinai, where He gave them the Ten Commandments. Today, we share in the New Covenant, which was offered to us through Jesus. Through Him, new promises were given to us;, promises of eternal life upon following Jesus. Below are some questions you should ask yourself before you start studying this section in detail.

1. What does it mean to move from glory to glory? You should seek to understand the literal meaning of these statements as well as its deeper meaning **(2 Corinthians 3:9)**.

2. What is your understanding of glory? Do you believe that being set free from the law means being elevated to a higher glory of Righteousness?

Romans 8:3-4 (NKJV)
(CHRIST Fulfills the Law)

(I did not come to abolish the Law; I come to fulfill the Law)

1 Peter 2:24

(Christ bore our sins in His body, that we might Live)

[24]*He personally carried our sins in his body on the cross so that we can be dead to sin and live for what is right. By his wounds you are healed.*

Romans 8:5-8 (NKJV)

(Carnal minded is death and you are against God and cannot please Him)

For those who live according to the flesh set their minds on the things of the flesh, but those who live according to the Spirit, the things of the Spirit. For to be carnally minded is death, but to be spiritually minded is life and peace. Because the carnal mind is enmity against God; for it is not subject to the law of God, nor indeed can be. 8 So then, those who are in the flesh cannot please God.

II Corinthians 3:17 (NKJV)

(There is Liberty in the Spirit)

Now the Lord is the Spirit; and where the Spirit of the Lord is, there is liberty.

II Corinthians 3:4-6 (NKJV)

(Ministers of the New Covenant)

And we have such trust through Christ toward God. Not that we are sufficient of ourselves to think of anything as being from ourselves, but our sufficiency is from God, who also made us sufficient as Ministers of the New Covenant, not of the letter but of the Spirit; for the letter kills, but the Spirit gives life.

2 Corinthians 3:7-18 (NKJV)

(Glory of the New Covenant)

But if the ministry of death, written and engraved on stones, was glorious, so that the children of Israel could not look steadily at the face of Moses because of the glory of his countenance, which glory was passing away, how will the ministry of the Spirit not be more glorious? For if the ministry of condemnation had glory, the ministry of righteousness exceeds much more in glory. For even what was made glorious had no glory in this respect, because of the glory that excels. For if what is passing away was glorious, what remains is much more glorious. Therefore, since we have such hope, we use great boldness of speech—unlike Moses, who put a veil over his face so that the children of Israel could not look steadily at the end of what was passing away. But their minds were blinded. For until this day the same veil remains uplifted in the reading of the Old Testament, because the veil is taken away in Christ. But even to this day, when Moses is read, a veil lies on their heart. Nevertheless when one turns to the Lord, the veil is taken away. Now the Lord is the Spirit; and where the Spirit of the Lord is, there is liberty. But we all, with unveiled face, beholding as in a mirror the glory of the Lord, are being transformed into the same image from glory to glory, just as by the Spirit of the Lord.

Philippians 1:11 (NKJV)

(Righteousness fruits through Christ to the GLORY of God!!)

Being filled with the fruits of righteousness which are given by Jesus Christ, to the glory and praise of God.

These readings reveal to us how we had been blind despite following the law. We followed the law blindly without knowing what was required of us (2 Corinthians 3:14; NKJV). When Jesus came on earth, a veil which hindered us from understanding the Law of Moses was removed, and now we can better understand what it means to follow God's commandments in love (John 14:15; NKJV). The Law is no longer forced on us but rather, it is written on our hearts (Hebrews 10:16; NKJV). We now have the will and the desire to do good deeds for the sake of God's glory.

The Bible teaches us that even in today's society, they will still want to operate under the law, when they hear it being spoken, even though Christ has come and removed the veil of the law from us. Moses hid his face with a veil when the glory was starting to dissipate to make room for the future Glory to come which is Jesus Christ—which is the greater Glory of the two.

Corinthians 3:13-18 (NKJV)

(The Glory of the Law Changes to The Glory of God in Jesus Christ, where now the Spirit gives us Liberty)

Unlike Moses, who put a veil over his face so that the children of Israel could not look steadily at the end of what was passing away. But their minds were blinded. For until this day the same veil remains unlifted in the reading of the Old Testament, because the veil is taken away in CHRIST. But even to this day, when Moses is read, a Veil Lies on their heart. Nevertheless when one turns to the Lord, the Veil is Taken Away. Now the Lord is the Spirit; and where the SPIRIT of the LORD is, there is LIBERTY. But we all, with unveiled face, beholding as in a mirror the GLORY of the Lord, are being transformed into the same image from GLORY to GLORY, just as by the Spirit of the Lord.

Now, in this New Glory of the Spirit in Jesus Christ, the written law (Romans 10:4 NKJV) is removed, and we become the Ministers of the New Covenant. This means the law and rules were written by men inspired by God for us to follow. Now, our lifestyles led by the Spirit of God should become the living Epistle for all to read. This Spirit-led lifestyle change takes us from Glory of reading the law to be right with God, to the Glory of reading our lifestyles in the Spirit of Christ, who makes us Right with God!

This is from GLORY to GLORY

(Read the verses on the next page; it will explain From Glory to Glory in Scriptures)

2 Corinthians 3:1-6 (NKJV)

(Christ's Epistle)

Do we begin again to commend ourselves? Or do we need, as some others, epistles of commendation to you or letters of commendation from you? [2] You are our epistle written in our hearts, known and read by all men; [3]clearly you are an epistle of Christ, ministered by us, written not with ink but by the Spirit of the living God, not on tablets of stone but on tablets of flesh, that is, of the heart.

The Spirit, Not the Letter

And[4] we have such trust through Christ toward God. [5] Not that we are sufficient of ourselves to think of anything as being from ourselves, but our sufficiency is from God, [6] who also made us sufficient as ministers of the new covenant, not of the letter but of the [a]Spirit; for the letter kills, but the Spirit gives life.

Now, you should expect to have a better understanding of what moving from glory to glory means. You should also be able to appreciate what Jesus did for us by dying on the cross and how that helped us move **From Glory to Glory.**

Meditate on your life and think about how good it is to live a free life, where you are offered several chances to make right your mistakes.

Chapter 5
"ARE CHRISTIANS UNDER THE LAW?"

Initially, man lived by the law and all his ways were made right by the law. If the law found any fault in a man, he deserved to be punished. When Jesus redeemed us from sin, He redeemed us from the law too. We are no longer bound by the law; WE ARE BOUND by His LOVE. We are not to judge one another by law rather we should correct each other in love and let God do the judging.

This section should be covered in the 6th week of studying this book. It introduces the topic of the book, explaining why righteousness cannot and should not be measured by the law. Righteousness, according to this section, means accepting what Jesus has done to make us right with God. His commandments were given to us to guide us and be a schoolmaster until Jesus came (Galatians 3:24). Jesus summed up all the commandments to one commandment of love. With love, all other laws become irrelevant. This is because it is hard for one to wrong others when they love them. It is also hard for someone who loves God to hate His people. Also, it is hard for someone to break God's commandments if they love Him (John 14:15). While reading through this section, think about the following:

1. Are there any rules which you find too stringent to follow? Mention them.

2. Do you think if people treated each other with love, the law would be necessary?

3. Have you ever experienced a situation where love superseded all set laws?

THE LAW IS FOR THE UNBELIEVING SINNERS.

1 Timothy 1:9; KJV
(Law is Not made for a righteous man)

Knowing this, that the law is not made for a righteous man, but for the lawless and disobedient, for the ungodly and for sinners, for unholy and profane, for murderers of fathers and murderers of mothers, for manslayers,

Remember, we all have righteousness because of Jesus's death and resurrection to remove the law for righteousness' sake (Romans 10:4) (Colossians 2:14).

1 Corinthians 6:9-11 AMP
(But such were some of you)

9 Do you not know that the unrighteous will not inherit or have any share in the kingdom of God? Do not be deceived; neither the sexually immoral, nor idolaters,

10 nor adulterers, nor (perversely) effeminate, nor homosexuals, nor thieves, nor the greedy, nor drunkards, nor revilers [whose words are used as weapons to abuse, insult, humiliate, intimidate, or slander], nor swindlers will inherit or have any share in the kingdom of God.

11 And SUCH WERE SOME OF YOU [BEFORE YOU BELIEVED]. But you were WASHED [by the ATONING SACRIFICE OF CHRIST], you WERE SANCTIFIED [set apart for God, and made holy], you were justified [DECLARED FREE OF GUILT] in the name of the Lord Jesus Christ and in the [Holy] Spirit of our God [the source of the believer's new life and changed behavior].Remember, we all have righteousness because of Jesus's death and resurrection to remove the law for righteousness' sake (Romans 10:4) (Colossians 2:14).

Romans 3:19; KJV

Now we know that what things so ever the law saith, it saith to them who are under the law: that every mouth may be stopped, and all the world may become guilty before God.

Christian are not under the law anymore because of Christ.

Romans 10:4; KJV

For Christ is the end of the law for righteousness to everyone that believeth.

In 1 Timothy 1:9 (KJV), the *"law is not made for a righteous man."*

 Romans 10:4 (KJV) shows that we are righteous and not under the law if we believe and have faith in Christ.

Romans 6:14; KJV

For sin shall not have dominion over you: for ye are not under the law, but under grace.

Now that the Law has been removed from us, we are under grace, and sin cannot condemn us anymore. By Christ, this Grace redeems us from the curse that the law produces and that kept us under bondage.

What Is The Purpose of The Law?

(**Romans 4:15**) The Law produces wrath

(**Romans 3:19**) So all can become guilty of sin to God

(**Galatians 3:22**) So that all can be confined under sin.

(**Galatian 3:19**) AND keep us bonded under sin till Jesus came

(**Galatians 3:23**) To be a guard, until faith was revealed. (**Galatians 3: 24**) The purpose of the law is to be a tutor to bring us to Christ, to be justified by faith.

The Law's Original Purpose was to be a Tutor For Us until Faith came; in other words, Until Jesus Came (Gal. 3:24).

Galatians 3:23-25 (NKJV)

²³*But before Faith came, we were kept under guard by the law, kept for the Faith, which would afterward be revealed.* ²⁴ *Therefore, the law was our tutor to bring us to Christ, that we might be Justified by Faith.* ²⁵ *But after Faith has come, We Are No Longer under a Tutor.*

Who is the Law for?

The law is not for the righteous, it is for sinners who have not received Christ (the unrighteous) (1 Timothy 1: 9 Amp). (1 Corinthians 6:9-11 Amp)

Why are we not under the law? Scriptures Below (AMP VERSION)

Galatians 2:18-21 AMP

(Because OBSERVING THE LAW IS NOT ESSENTIAL FOR SALVATION)

18 For if I [or anyone else should] REBUILD [THROUGH WORD or by PRACTICE] what I once tore down [the BELIEF THAT OBSERVING the LAW is ESSENTIAL for SALVATION], I prove myself to be a transgressor.

19 For through the Law I died to the Law and its demands on me [because SALVATION is provided through the DEATH and RESURRECTION of CHRIST], so that I might [from now on] live to God.

20 I have been crucified with Christ [that is, in Him I have shared His crucifixion]; it is no longer I who live, but Christ lives in me. The life I now live in the body I live by faith [by adhering to, relying on, and completely trusting] in the Son of God, who loved me and gave Himself up for me.

21 I do not ignore or nullify the [GRACIOUS GIFT of the] GRACE of GOD [His amazing, UNMERITED FAVOR], for if RIGHTEOUSNESS comes through [OBSERVING] the LAW, then CHRIST DIED NEEDLESSLY. [His suffering and death would have had no purpose whatsoever.]"

Because Keeping the law is not Essential for Salvation (Galatians 2: 18-21 AMP)

Why are we not under the law?

Because the law increased sin in us (*Romans 5:20*)

Because we needed to be delivered from sin (*Romans 8:2*)

Because Christ Fulfilled it. (*Mathew 5:17*) (*Rom 8:3-4*)

(1 Peter 2:24)

So sin will not have dominion over us (*Romans 6:14*)

To take us from the works of the law for Righteousness (**Deut. 6:25**)

Because the Bible says no one can be made righteous or justified by works of the Law. (*Galatian 2:16*)(*Romans 3:18*)

Because the righteousness of God is not by the law; it is by Christ.(*Romans 3:21-22*)

So we can obtain Salvation through the Blood Sacrifice of Christ So that we can obtain a righteous standing with God until Salvation that doesn't come from the law emerges (*Romans 3:23-28*).

What are the benefits of not being under the law and Being in Christ?

We are justified in God's eyes through Jesus.(**Galatians 2:26**)

So we can receive the RIGHTEOUSNESS of God through

Christ.(**Romans 10:3; Romans 3:21-22**)

So that we would be made righteous in God's eyes (*Romans 8:4*)

Because the flesh was made weak by the law.(**Romans 8:3**)

Because the law cannot make you righteous.

Removed enmity and abolished the law of commandments.(**Ephesians 2: 15**)

 So you would not be condemned). (<u>**Romans**</u> <u>**8:1**</u>) , <u>**Galatians 2:16**</u>)

So we can be Redeemed from the curses. (<u>**Galatians 3:13**</u>)

So you can live free. (<u>**Romans 8:20**</u>)

So that all the promises of God gave us would be yes. (<u>**2 Corinthians 1:20**</u>)

So that the blessings of Abraham will be ours. (<u>**Galatians**</u> <u>3</u>:14)

So we can have Salvation apart from the law (**Romans 3:2328,** <u>**John**</u> <u>**5:39-40**</u>)

So we can go into the Holiest of all Places (**Hebrews 10:17-19**)

Since Jesus said He didn't abolish the law and it won't disappear (<u>**Matthew**</u> <u>**5: 17-18**</u>), do we still teach the Law of Moses? Not for works unto Righteousness or Salvation!!!

(<u>Romans 10:4</u>(, 1 <u>Timothy 1:5-7</u>)

Reading through this section, you will learn that Jesus came on earth not to judge us but to redeem us from our sinful nature. He taught us not to judge each other but to love each other. The Law was mainly made up of stringent rules which had strict punishments, if broken, but. when Jesus came, He denounced these laws, giving us freedom from them to become in right standing with God. **"After the Cross,"** Christ gave us a sin removal place in Him.

Okay, I now know I'm free from the law, what do I do next?

Accept by faith, the Righteousness of God unto Salvation, which comes through Jesus Christ, which makes us pure and holy. (1 Corinthians 1:30)

The Law is no good for Righteousness (Romans 3:20 -28) However, if you try to use the law to be justified, you will fall from grace. (Galatians 5:4)

Romans 4:15

(Law produces wrath)

For the Law produces wrath. Now where there is no Law, neither can there be any violation of it.

Colossians 2:14

(Canceled written code)

Having canceled the written code"(is the law)", with its regulations, that was against us and that stood opposed to us; he took it away, nailing it to the cross.

Romans 7:7-12 (NKJV)

(Sin's Advantage in the Law)

What shall we say then? Is the law sin? Certainly not! On the contrary, I would not have known sin except through the law. For I would not have known covetousness unless the law had said, "You shall not covet." But sin, taking opportunity by the commandment, produced in me all manner of evil desire. For apart from the law sin was dead. I was alive once without the law, but when the commandment came, sin revived and I died. And the commandment, which was to bring life, I found to bring death. For sin, taking occasion by the commandment, deceived me, and by it killed me. Therefore the law is holy, and the commandment holy and just and good.

In *Deuteronomy 28,* It shows that if you keep all of these laws you will receive all of these blessing. However, if you don't keep all these laws you will be cursed. Galatians 3:13-14 shows that Jesus has redeemed us from those curses.

Christ hath redeemed us from the curse of the law, being made a curse for us: for it is written, Cursed is every one that hanged on a tree: That the blessing of Abraham might come on the Gentiles through Jesus Christ; that we might receive the promise of the Spirit through faith.

In the Old Covenant under the law, their righteousness was given to them by keeping the law.

Deuteronomy 6:25

(They had to work for it)

And it shall be our righteousness, if we observe to do all these commandments before the Lord our God, as he hath commanded us.

While in the New Covenant, your righteousness comes by faith in Jesus Christ. You don't work for it

Luke 22:20; NIV*" *(Jesus talking),* "*This cup is the new covenant in my blood, which is poured out for you.*

Ephesians 2:8-10 (NKJV)

(Not By works)

For by grace you have been saved through faith, and that not of yourselves; it is the gift of God, not of works, lest anyone should boast. For we are His

workmanship, created in Christ Jesus for good works, which God prepared beforehand that we should walk in them.

Romans 10:4 (KJV)

For Christ is the end of the law for righteousness to everyone that believeth.

Christ gave His life so we could be placed under the blood of the New Covenant of Christ. Now by faith, we receive Grace and Righteousness through Jesus.

Hallelujah!!! Not by works of the law that we had to do from the Old Covenant, but by blood of Jesus in the New Covenant where He did the work for us. We have now been set free from sin (Romans 8:1-4(, Romans 6:14) and set free from the law (Romans 10:4) and also delivered from the curses of the law (Galatians 3: 13-14).

I'll give you an example of this usage in the Bible. JESUS shows us in Mathew 5: 17-20: We are now "Ministers of a New Covenant" not of the law, because the law kills!!!

Matthew 5:17-20; NKJV

(Break and teach others to break the Law, you will be ranked least in the Kingdom of Heaven)

"*Do not think that I came to destroy the Law or the Prophets. I did not come to destroy but to fulfill. For assuredly, I say to you, till heaven and earth pass away, one jot or one tittle will by no means pass from the law till all is fulfilled. Whoever therefore breaks one of the least of these commandments, and teaches men so, shall be called least in the kingdom of heaven; but whoever does and teaches them, he shall be called great in the kingdom of heaven. For I say to you, that unless your Righteousness exceeds the Righteousness of the scribes and Pharisees (**The Phar-**

isees righteousness was Deut. 625), you will by no means enter the kingdom of heaven.

Deuteronomy 6:25 NKJV

(Pharisees Righteousness)

Then it will be righteousness for us, if we are careful to observe all these commandments before the Lord our God, as He has commanded us.

The Pharisees' Righteousness was to keep the law to gain their Right Standing with God.

As you see in **Mathew 5:19,** Christ's Judgment treated the one who is breaking the laws but did not condemn him to eternal death; they still enter into the Kingdom of Heaven. However, they will be ranked least in the Kingdom of Heaven.

Christ has made us right with God by removing our sins from us!!! hallelujah!!

The law is no good for righteousness with God!!

II Corinthians 3:7-9; NKJV

(The law is the Ministry of Death and Condemnation)

But if the ministry of death, written and engraved on stones(Law was written on stone), was glorious, so that the children of Israel could not look steadily at the face of Moses because of the glory of his countenance, which glory was passing away, how will the ministry of the Spirit not be more glorious? For if the ministry of condemnation had glory, the ministry of righteousness exceeds much more in glory."

I Corinthians 15:55-57; NKJV

(Strength of Sin is the Law)

55 O Death, where is your sting? O Hades, where is your victory?

56 The sting of death is sin, and the strength of sin is the law. 57But thanks be to God, who gives us the victory through our Lord Jesus Christ.

Romans 3:21-23; NKJV

(GOD'S RIGHTEOUSNESS is apart from the Law)

But now the righteousness of God apart from the law is revealed, being witnessed by the Law and the Prophets, even the righteousness of God, through faith in Jesus Christ, to all and on all who believe. For there is no difference; for all have a sinned and fall short of the Glory of God.

A lot of people have not accepted God's righteousness because they still have the veil of Moses over their faces (2 Cor. 3:14-17) when it comes to the law and have not accepted the Righteousness of God because they keep trying to establish their own.

Romans 10:3-4; NKJV

(GOD'S RIGHTEOUSNESS is through Christ Jesus)

II Corinthians 3:14-17; NKJV

(The veil of Moses has them blinded when it comes to the Law)

[14]"But their minds were blinded. For until this day the same veil remains unlifted in the reading of the Old Testament, because the veil is taken away in Christ. [15] But even to this day, when Moses is read, a veil lies on their heart. [16]Nevertheless,

when one turns to the Lord, the veil is taken away. [17]*Now the Lord is the Spirit; and where the Spirit of the Lord is, there is liberty.*"

The Bible teaches us that 'Teachers of the Law' do not know what they are doing, because we are Ministers of the New Covenant of the Spirit of Righteousness. We have now become teachers of the good news, which is that our sins have been paid for through the death and resurrection of Christ for us to have righteousness or in other words, we are in right standing with god!!!

1 Timothy 1:6-7; NKJV

(Teachers of the law know not what they do)

[6]*from which some, having strayed, have turned aside to idle talk, desiring to be teachers of the law,* [7]*understanding neither what they say nor the things which they affirm.*"

(Galatians 5:2-5; NKJV)

(You have fallen from Grace, trying to keep the Law)

[2]*"Indeed I, Paul, say to you that if you become circumcised, Christ will profit you nothing.* [3]*And I testify again to every man who becomes circumcised that he is a debtor to keep the whole law.* [4]*You have become estranged from Christ, you who attempt to be justified by law; you have fallen from grace.* [5]*For we through the Spirit eagerly wait for the hope of righteousness by faith.*"

Hebrews 8: 8-13; NKJV

(A new Covenant is given)

"Because finding fault with them, He says: "Behold, the days are coming, says the Lord, when I will make a new covenant with the house of Israel and with

the house of Judah—not according to the covenant that I made with their fathers in the day when I took them by the hand to lead them out of the land of Egypt; because they did not continue in My covenant, and I disregarded them, says the Lord. For this is the covenant that I will make with the house of Israel after those days, says the Lord: I will put My laws in their mind and write them on their hearts; and I will be their God, and they shall be My people. None of them shall teach his neighbor, and none his brother, saying, 'Know the Lord,' for all shall know Me, from the least of them to the greatest of them. For I will be merciful to their unrighteousness, and their sins and their lawless deeds I will remember no more." In that He says, "A NEW COVENANT," He has made The First COVENANT Obsolete. Now what is becomingObsolete and growing old is ready to vanish away."

Here, he is talking about the law becoming obsolete and presently obsolete. However, some still have the veil of Moses over their eyes when it comes to the laws of the Old Covenant

(Ministers of the New Covenant)

II Corinthians 3:4-6; NKJV

(Ministers of the New Covenant)

And we have such trust through Christ toward God. Not that we are sufficient of ourselves to think of anything as being from ourselves, but our sufficiency is from God, who also made us sufficient as ministers of the new covenant, not of the letter but of the Spirit; for the letter kills, but the Spirit gives life.

II Corinthians 3:7-9; NKJV

(Law engraved in Stone, ministry of death)

and the Ministry of the Spirit of life **Righteousness** is revealed) "But if the ministry of death, written and engraved on stones, was glorious, so that the children of Israel could not look steadily at the face of Moses because of the glory of his countenance, which glory was passing away, how will the ministry of the Spirit not be more glorious? For if the ministry of condemnation had glory, the ministry of righteousness exceeds much more in glory."

THANK GOD; HALLELUJAH!!!! YOU HAVE BEEN SET FREE!!!

If you believe in the Scriptures, study them, and you will be free, because all Scriptures are given for reproof, correction, and for instruction in righteousness.

P.S. This doesn't give you the right to just go out and sin because you have been delivered by grace.

Romans 6:1-2; KJV
(God Forbid continuance in sin)

What shall we say then? Shall we continue in sin, that grace may abound? GOD FORBID! (It is forbidden by God!) How shall we, that are dead to sin, live any longer therein?

If there is anyone who is reading this and you want to receive the blessing of salvation, forgiveness of sins, and removal of curses from your life, and you don't know Jesus Christ, read Romans 10:8-13 and say this out loud.

***I confess with my mouth that the Lord Jesus is my Lord and Savior; I ask God to forgive all my sins, and I believe in my heart that God raised Him from the dead, and now, I believe I am saved. Amen. ***

Romans 10:10 - *For with the heart man believeth unto righteousness; and with the mouth, confession is made unto salvation.* (**Find a Bible-teaching church to continue your glorious walk with Jesus. I leave you with Romans; this just reaffirms what I have been teaching.**

"Romans 3:18-28; KJV"

Therefore by the deeds of the law there shall no flesh be justified in his sight: for by the law is the knowledge of sin. But now the righteousness of God without the law is manifested, being witnessed by the law and the prophets; Even the righteousness of God which is by faith of Jesus Christ unto all and upon all them that believe: for there is no difference: For all have sinned, and come short of the glory of God; being justified freely by his grace through the redemption that is in Christ Jesus: Whom God hath set forth to be a propitiation (turning away of wrath by an offering) through faith in his blood, to declare his righteousness for the remission of sins that are past, through the forbearance of God; to declare, I say, at this time his righteousness: that he might be just, and the justifier of him which believeth in Jesus. Where is boasting then? It is excluded. By what law? Of works. Nay: but by the law of faith. Therefore we conclude that a man is justified by faith without the deeds of the law.

Galatians 3:10-12; NKJV

(Cursed anyone continuing in the law)

For as many as are of the works of the law are under the curse; for it is written, "Cursed is everyone who does not continue in all things which are written in the book of the law, to do them." But that no one is justified by the law in the sight of God is evident, for "the just shall live by faith." Yet the law is not of faith, but "the man who does them shall live by them.

But now, God sent His son to take away the curse and the law for Righteousness and make us sons and daughters of God.

Galatians 4:4-5; NKJV

(At the fullness of times, God redeemed us from the law and made us sons & daughters)

"But when the fullness of the time had come, God sent forth His Son, born of a woman, born under the law, to redeem those who were under the law, that we might receive the adoption as sons."

Are You a True son of God or does Satan still trick you?

Have you truly accepted His gift of Righteousness through Christ's suffering by Faith?

Or have you left the spiritual part of Righteousness behind the one that God gives and you are trying to establish your own?

The Law's Original Purpose was to be a Tutor for Us until Faith came. In other words, until Jesus Came (Gal. 3:24) "Therefore, anyone breaking the rules or laws would be under a Curse."

But now, God sent His Son to take away the curse and the law for Righteousness (Gal. 3:13), and make us sons and daughters of God (Gal.4:4-5)

*So that the righteous requirement of the law might be fulfilled in us. (**Romans 8: 3-4**)*

Chapter 6
How do You Detox from
the Law into Jesus Christ?

SALVATION IS NOT BY THE LAW;
IT'S BY JESUS CHRIST ALONE! (John 6:63)

(No One is justified by the Law. Justification is only in Christ Jesus!) Galatians 2:16 (NKJV)

[16] *knowing that a man is not [a]justified by the works of the law but by faith in Jesus Christ, even we have believed in Christ Jesus, that we might be justified by faith in Christ and not by the works of the law; for by the works of the law no flesh shall be Justified.*

So, if anyone is trying to get you justified with God by rules, regulations, and laws through smooth words, they are deceiving you and will become a stumbling block to you.

Romans 14:5-23

(Let no man be a stumbling block by what they tell you to do or not to do for God)

Romans 14: 23, Do not cause your brother to stumble by what he eats, drink or anything else that causes him to stumble.

Even if someone doesn't believe in what Christ has done for them, we cannot be their stumbling block. By trying to force the message down their throat, this could cause them to fall further away from God.

One of the most important things we have to look at first is **Detox**. A lot of times, we have to be **detoxed**. Like the Pharisees did when Jesus first came;, they did not believe Him, and they claimed He was blasphemous against Moses and God.

Acts 6:11 (NKJV)

Then they secretly induced men to say, "We have heard him speak blasphemous words against Moses and God.

As a matter of fact, most of the Pharisees and Sadducees kept the Veil of Moses over their eyes

2 Corinthians 3:14-16 (NKJV)

But their minds were blinded. For until this day the same veil remains unlifted in the reading of the Old Testament, because the veil is taken away in Christ. But even to this day, when Moses is read, a veil lies on their heart. Nevertheless when one turns to the Lord, the veil is taken away.

They still did not believe IN CHRIST'S TEACHINGS when it came to the laws, instead, they pitched their tents with the laws that Moses gave them and that's the veil that 2nd Corinthians is talking about. Most people still believe that to be right with God, you have to follow the handwritten ordinance of God to be right with Him. You don't! As it is explained in **Colossians 2: 14 (NKJV):** *having wiped out the handwriting of requirements that was against us, which was contrary to us. And He has taken it out of the way, having nailed it to the cross.*

There is a reason to keep the law. However, it is not to be right with God! I will explain this in detail later in this book.

Colossians 2:4-23 (KJV) (Read)
Colossians 2: 4-7
(Do not let them deceive you with enticing words)

And this I say, lest any man should beguile you with enticing words. For though I be absent in the flesh, yet am I with you in the spirit, joying and beholding your order, and the steadfastness of your faith in Christ. As ye have therefore received Christ Jesus the Lord, so walk ye in him: Rooted and built up in him, and established in the faith, as ye have been taught, abounding therein with thanksgiving.

Colossians 2:8-10 (NKJV)

(Don't let anyone trick you with vain philosophy)

Beware lest anyone cheat you through philosophy and empty deceit, according to the tradition of men, according to the basic principles of the world, and not according to Christ. For in Him dwells all the fullness of the Godhead bodily; and you are complete in Him, who is the head of all principality and power.

We are complete in Jesus; He fulfilled what we needed to be complete.

Colossians 2:11-14, 23 (NKJV)

11 In whom also ye are circumcised with the circumcision made without hands, in putting off the body of the sins of the flesh by the circumcision of Christ:

12 Buried with him in baptism, wherein also ye are risen with him through the faith of the operation of God, who hath raised him from the dead.

13 And you, being dead in your sins and the uncircumcision of your flesh, hath he quickened together with him, having forgiven you all trespasses;

14 Blotting out the handwriting of ordinances that was against us, which was contrary to us, and took it out of the way, nailing it to his cross;

Colossians 2:15-17, (NKJV) *The ordinance of the Law was nailed to the Cross and Jesus removed it from us. He didn't take it because it was no good; He took it because it was perfect and we could not keep it.*

15 And having spoiled principalities and powers, he made a shew of them openly, triumphing over them in it.

16 Let no man therefore judge you in meat, or in drink, or in respect of an holyday, or of the new moon, or of the Sabbath days:

17 Which are a shadow of things to come; but the body is of Christ.

We have to understand that God did us an awesome favor by sending Christ to die for us. Now, as to the law and when and how we celebrate these days, whether we celebrate on Saturday or Sunday, are only shadows of things to come.

Colossians 2:18-23, (NKJV)

18 Let no man beguile you of your reward in a voluntary humility and worshipping of angels, intruding into those things which he hath not seen, vainly puffed up by his fleshly mind,

19 And not holding the Head, from which all the body by joints and bands having nourishment ministered, and knit together, increased with the increase of God.

20 Wherefore if ye be dead with Christ from the rudiments of the world, why, as though living in the world, are ye subject to ordinances,

21 (Touch not; taste not; handle not;

22 Which all are to perish with the using;) after the commandments and doctrines of men?

23 Which things have indeed a shew of wisdom in will worship, and humility, and neglecting of the body: not in any honour to the satisfying of the flesh.

Now, Finish and Completely DETOX from the Law! I will give you these scriptures to help you Detox from the LAW Completely. Study these next scriptures, they will help you DETOX FROM THE LAW.

Ephesians 2:14-16 (NLT)

For Christ he has brought peace to us. He united Jews and Gentiles into one people when, in his own body on the cross, he broke down the wall of hostility that separated us. 15 He did this by ending the system of law with its commandments and regulations. He made peace between Jews and Gentiles by creating in himself one new people from the two groups. 16 Together as one body, Christ reconciled both groups to God by means of his death on the cross, and our hostility toward each other was put to death.

Romans 10:4 (NKJV)

⁴*For Christ is the end of the law for righteousness to everyone who believes.*

Galatians 2:15-16 (NKJV)

15 *We who are Jews by nature, and not sinners of the Gentiles,* ¹⁶*knowing that a man is not justified by the works of the law but by faith in Jesus Christ, even we have believed in Christ Jesus, that we might be justified by faith in Christ and not by the works of the law; for by the works of the law no flesh shall be justified.*

Galatians 3:13 (NKJV)

¹³ *Christ has redeemed us from the curse of the law, having become a curse for us (for it is written, "Cursed is everyone who hangs on a tree"),*

Romans 3:21-24 (NKJV)

God's Righteousness through Faith

²¹*But now the righteousness of God apart from the law is revealed, being witnessed by the Law and the Prophets,* ²²*even the righteousness of God, through faith in Jesus Christ, to all and on all who believe. For there is no difference;* ²³*for all have sinned and fall short of the glory of God,* ²⁴*being justified freely by His grace through the redemption that is in Christ Jesus,*

Romans 3:25-28 (NKJV)

²⁵*whom God set forth as a propitiation by His blood, through faith, to demonstrate His righteousness, because in His forbearance God had passed over the sins that were previously committed,* ²⁶*to demonstrate at the present time His righteousness, that He might be just and the justifier of the one who has faith in Jesus.*

Romans 3:25-28 (NKJV)(Boasting Excluded)

²⁷*Where is boasting then? It is excluded. By what law? Of works? No,*

but by the law of faith. [28]Therefore we conclude that a man is justified by faith apart from the deeds of the law.

Colossians 2:14-15 (NKJV)

Having wiped out the handwriting of requirements that was against us, which was contrary to us. And He has taken it out of the way, having nailed it to the cross. [15]Having disarmed principalities and powers, He made a public spectacle of them, triumphing over them in it.

Romans 3:19-20 (NKJV)

Now we know that whatever the law says, it says to those who are under the law, that every mouth may be stopped, and all the world may become guilty before God. [20] Therefore by the deeds of the law no flesh will be justified in His sight, for by the law is the knowledge of sin.

Romans 3:10 (NKJV)

As it is written: "There is none righteous, no, not one;

Romans 3:23-25 (NKJV)

[23]for all have sinned and fall short of the glory of God, [24]being justified freely by His grace through the redemption that is in Christ Jesus, [25]whom God set forth as a propitiation by His blood, through faith, to demonstrate His righteousness, because in His forbearance God had passed over the sins that were previously committed,

Chapter 7
What is the Gospel of Jesus Christ?

John 12:47 (NIV)

If anyone hears my words but does not keep them, I do not judge that person. For I did not come to judge the world, but to save the world.

Galatians 1:15-16; Romans 10:9-10; John 12:47 (NKJV); Galatians 1:68 (NKJV); Galatians 1:11-12 (NKJV); Acts 20:24 (NKJV); Galatians 1:15-16; Romans 1:16-17 (NKJV).

All these readings above portray the importance of the gospel of Christ in our lives as Christians. The works that Jesus did on the earth are revisited in the gospel, as well as the teachings of His disciples. We are encouraged to follow in His footsteps and to shun sin and the law. Jesus came on earth not to judge us but to save us from our sins (John 12:47; NKJV).

Our sins were, therefore, cleansed and the punishments which were prescribed by law for our sins were erased and replaced with promises of blessings. To claim these blessings, we have to receive what Christ has done for us "After the Cross." He accomplished this by fulfilling the Laws for Us

(Romans 8: 1-2). We are obliged to love one another and live in harmony. Love conquers the law because, with love, no one will have the intentions to do something that will hurt or offend another person. Jesus gave a commandment, "Love your neighbor as yourself"

John 15:12 (NKJV)

This is My commandment, that you love one another as I have loved you.

Professor Yarborough spoke that in the 1900s, thirty percent of Americans were Christians. He said now, the number of Christians America have is below 15%.

Why? Let's look at the Gospels we are preaching.

The Ministry of Righteousness: Let's look at what Paul preached. He said if we are preaching anything else, we are accursed.

WHAT DOES PAUL CONSIDER ANOTHER GOSPEL?

Galatians 1:6-8; NKJV

(Accursed to speak any other Gospel)

[6]*I marvel that you are turning away so soon from Him who called you in **the GRACE of Christ**, to a different gospel, <u>Which</u>[7] <u>is Not Another</u>; but there are some who trouble you and want **to Pervert the Gospel of Christ**. But[8] even if we, or an angel from heaven, preach any other gospel to you than what we have preached to you, let him be accursed."*

What is not REVEALED is that Paul said so profoundly that there is a Gospel that can put you under a curse. By stating so profoundly, he said, "It is not another Gospel." "They are using the same Gospel to take you out of the 'Grace of Christ! They have perverted the Gospel of Christ!'" (Galatians 1:6-7; NKJV)

Satan has slithered his way into the church. Now, some churches are preaching curses on themselves and their people through the Law, and they don't know they are putting them into BONDAGE and are not setting them **free through Christ**. The Gospel that Paul says is swaying you away from Christ, is the same Gospel that is swaying you to Christ, except they are not rightfully dividing the truth. They are placing people back under the bondage Christ died and removed them from.

Paul stated in Galatians 1:6 that some have turned away from the Grace of Christ, into a perverted version of the Gospel. Any gospel that is not representing the Grace of Christ is another Gospel. Paul clearly puts real emphases on this truth when he says he doesn't care even if an angel from heaven bring another gospel; they shall be accursed too!

Ephesians 2:8-9 (NKJV)
(It is by GRACE through Faith you have been Saved)

For by "GRACE" you have been SAVED through FAITH, and that Not of YOURSELF; it is the GIFT of God, ⁹ Not of Works, lest anyone should boast.

Romans 3:24 (NLT)
(Christ freed us from the penalty of sin THROUGH GRACE)

Yet God, in his "GRACE", Freely makes us right in his sight. He did this through Christ Jesus when he Freed Us from the Penalty for Our Sins.

2 Timothy 2:15 (NKJV)

(Rightfully divide the truth)

[15] *Be diligent to present yourself approved to God, a worker who does not need to be ashamed, rightly dividing the word of truth.*

So, in the context of the truth, we see that if what they are teaching or preaching is anything other than the Grace of Christ or what Christ has done for you to make you right with God, such a one is under a curse, especially if they're trying to be right with God by your actions, 'the Law' (Romans 10:3}.)

Galatians 3:10-12; NKJV

(Cursed is anyone continuing in the law)

*"For as many as are of the **Works of the Law are under the Curse;** for it is written, "Cursed is everyone who does not continue in all things which are written in the book of the law, to do them." But that no one is justified by the law in the sight of God is evident, for "the just shall live by faith." Yet the Law is not of Faith, but "the man who does them shall live by them."*

No one is justified by the Law because the Law is not of Faith; it is from your works. The things you do to be justified with God or in other words, the things you do to be right with God, is not what God requires you to do through your works to be right with Him! God requires you to have faith in what Christ has done for you to be right with Him, which is, receiving the Grace of God that purified us through Jesus unto salvation and gives us the ability to say no to ungodliness and worldly passions (Romans 10:4, Romans 6:14, Titus 2:11-14;)

Romans 6:14; KJV

For sin shall not have dominion over you: for ye are not under the law, but under grace.

Titus 2:11-14 (NIV)

(God's Grace gives us Salvation)

[11]*For the Grace of God has appeared that offers salvation to all people.* [12] *It teaches us to say "No" to ungodliness and worldly passions, and to live self-controlled, upright and godly lives in this present age,* [13] *while we wait for the blessed hope—the appearing of the glory of our great God and Savior, Jesus Christ,* [14] *who gave himself for us to redeem us from all wickedness and to purify for himself a people that are his very own, eager to do what is good.*

Galatians 1:11-12 (NKJV)

(Gospel from Revelation of Christ)

[11]*"But I make known to you, brethren, that the gospel which was preached by me is not according to man.* [12]*For I neither received it from man, nor was I taught it, but it came through the "REVELATION of JESUS CHRIST."*

Now, we know the Bible shows us that Paul was taught by a man by the name of Gamaliel in Acts 22:3. However, when he proclaimed no man taught me this Gospel in Galatians 1:12, he got this one from Christ. We know from scriptures that the Gospel that Gamaliel taught him was the law. So, in other words, the law is not the same Gospel that Paul is preaching nor is it the same Gospel that Christ gave him.

(Gospel from the Revelation of Christ)

Galatians 1:15-16; NKJV

"(GOSPEL revealed is Christ in me)

¹⁵*But when it pleased God, who separated me from my mother's womb and called me through His grace, to REVEAL HIS SON IN ME, that I MIGHT PREACH HIM (CHRIST) among the Gentiles.*

WHAT IS THE GOSPEL OF CHRIST?

Romans 1:16-17; NKJV
(In the Gospel of Christ, the Righteousness of God is revealed)

In the Gospel of Jesus Christ in Romans 1:16-17, the Righteousness of God is revealed. This takes you from Faith in the law to Faith in what Christ has done for you.

This concept is all over the Bible; *HOWEVER.,* Satan has found a way of taking people back to what the Pharisees taught—the one thing that keeps them under curses (*GALATIANS* 3:1012)—the **LAW!!!**) AS Galatians 3:12 shows, **"The law is not of faith!"**

So, the Gospel that Paul preached had to do with Christ and not the Law!

Colossians 1:25-29 (NKJV)
(PRESENT everyone PERFECT IN JESUS CHRIST)

²⁵*of which I became a minister according to the stewardship from God which was given to me for you, to fulfill the word of God,* ²⁶*the mystery which has been hidden from ages and from generations, but now has been revealed to His saints.* ²⁷*To them God willed to make known what the riches of the glory of this mystery among the Gentiles are: which is Christ in you, the hope of glory.* ²⁸*Him*

we preach, warning every man and teaching every man in all wisdom, that
we may present every man perfect in Christ Jesus. ²⁹ To this end I also labor,
striving according to His working which works in me mightily.

So, in the Gospel of Christ is his righteousness revealed. It is "Christ
in *you*" to make everyone perfect in Jesus Christ!

How do we know we can use that (everyone is perfect in Jesus Christ,) or we
have the righteousness of Christ as a ministry to be right with god and not
the law to be right with god instead?

II Corinthians 3:10-11; NKJV

(Ministry of Righteousness)

For if the ministry of condemnation (Law) had glory, the ministry of righteousness exceeds much more in glory.

Philippians 3:9; NKJV
(Not Righteousness from the Law, but righteousness through faith in Christ)

And be found in Him, not having my own righteousness, which is from the law,
*but that which is **through faith in Christ**, the righteousness which is from God*
by faith.

Deut. 6:25 shows you your righteousness and not the righteousness of
Christ, which is by faith.

1 Timothy 1:6-7

(Teachers of the law know not what they do nor what they affirm)

from which some, having strayed, have turned aside to idle talk, desiring to be teachers of the law, understanding neither what they say nor the things which they affirm."

Romans 7:9

(Law made sin revived and I died)

⁹*"For apart from the law sin was dead. I was alive once without the law, but when the commandment came, sin revived, and I died. "*

Romans 7:10 (NKJV)

(Commandments bring death)

¹⁰ *And the commandment, (LAWS) which was to bring life, I found to bring death.*

In Galatians 1:6-8 (NKJV) Paul, already told us we are cursed if we preach any other gospel besides the one he's preaching.

Why is it we don't try to find out what Paul preached? Why has God hidden this from some and revealed it to others?

Deut. 28:15

(You are cursed if you break these commandments)

2 Corinthians 11:3-4 (NKJV)

³*But I fear, lest somehow, as the serpent deceived Eve by his craftiness, so your minds may be corrupted from the SIMPLICITY that is in "CHRIST". ⁴For if he who comes preaches another "JESUS" whom we have not preached, or if you receive a different spirit which you have not received, or a different gospel which you have not accepted—you may well put up with it!*

Galatians 1:6-8 (NKJV)

⁶I marvel that you are turning away so soon from Him who called you in the Grace of "CHRIST", to a different gospel, ⁷which is not another"; but there are some who trouble you and want to Pervert the Gospel of "CHRIST." ⁸But even if we, or an angel from heaven, preach any other gospel to you than what we have preached to you, Let Him be "ACCURSED".

Galatians 3:10-12 (NKJV)

(Cursed anyone continuing in the law)

¹⁰"For as many as are of the works of the law are under the curse; for it is written, "Cursed is everyone who does not continue in all things which are written in the book of the law, to do them." ¹¹But that no one is justified by the law in the sight of God is evident, for "the just shall live by faith." ¹²Yet the law is not of faith, but "the man who does them shall live by them."

A lot of churches are teaching the laws of God in their church to keep people in control and are not teaching what Paul was teaching, the Righteousness of God. Even though they have good intentions: they are keeping them under the curses Christ came to remove.

The law was only given as a tutor till Christ came. The Law was so perfect (**Psalms 19:7**) that God knew no man could keep it. So, he sent the law to teach and keep you in confinement.

Galatians 3:24 (NKJV)

(The Law was only given as a tutor till Christ came.)

²⁴ Therefore the law was our tutor to bring us to Christ, that we might be justified by faith."

God's righteousness comes through faith in Jesus Christ," not through works of the Law. So, if we are teaching people to be right with God through the Law and not via Christ inside of them that makes them right with God, then we are preaching another Gospel besides what Paul preached. Then there could be a curse on the teachings.

Romans 3:21-24 (NKJV) (#1-3)

(God's Righteousness through Faith)

²¹**But now the** righteousness of God apart from the law is revealed, **being witnessed by the Law and the Prophets,** ²²**even** the righteousness of God, through faith in Jesus Christ,*to all and on all who believe. For, there is no difference;* ²³ *for all have sinned and fall short of the glory of God,* ²⁴*being justified freely by His grace through the redemption that is in Christ Jesus.*

God has made us ministers of the Gospel of Christ like Paul and not ministers of the law which are accursed according to Galatian 1:6-8, We are now Ministers of the New Covenant.

2 Corinthians 3:4-6 (NKJV)

(MINISTERS OF THE NEW COVENANT)

⁴*"And we have such trust* **through Christ** *toward God.* ⁵*Not that we are sufficient of ourselves to think of anything as being from ourselves, but our sufficiency is from God,* ⁶*who also made us sufficient as Ministers of the New Covenant, not of the letter but of the Spirit; for the letter kills, but the Spirit gives life."*

So if you're not teaching your people about what Christ has done for them and that he is in them for freedom from the law for Righteousness. You are preaching death (Curses) on your people and yourself and not freedom, because the law brings death; it does not make you right with God!

II Corinthians 3:7 (NKJV)

(Ministry of Death)

⁷But if the ministry of death, written and engraved on stones was glorious, so that the children of Israel could not look steadily at the face of Moses because of the glory of his countenance, which glory was passing away,….

II Corinthians 3: 9-11 (NKJV)

(Glory; we receive through Righteousness of Christ)

*For if the ministry of condemnation had glory, **the ministry of righteousness exceeds much more in glory**. For even what was made glorious had no glory in this respect, because of the glory that excels. For if what is passing away was glorious, what remains is much more glorious."*

What most people don't understand is this. Your spiritual maturity is based on God revealing His Righteousness to you. As long as you are teaching about the laws, most of the time to be right with God and not His Righteousness, you are still on milk!!

Hebrews 5:12-13; NKJV

(Being on solid food and not milk is being skilled in Righteousness)

For though by this time you ought to be teachers, you need someone to TEACH you AGAIN the first PRINCIPLES of the ORACLE'S of GOD; and you have come to need milk and not solid food. For everyone who partakes only of milk is UNSKILLED in the word of RIGHTEOUSNESS, for he is a BABE."

This is the Gospel of Paul Which no man has given us, and through which God unveils the mystery of Christ in us!! As Paul stated in Galatian 1:15-16.

OUR MINISTRY IS TO REVEAL CHRIST IN US WHICH MAKES EVERY MAN PERFECT IN CHRIST

Colossians 1:25-29; NKJV

(PRESENT everyone PERFECT IN JESUS CHRIST)

I became a minister according to the stewardship from God which was given to me for you, to fulfill the word of God, the mystery which has been hidden from ages and from generations, but now has been revealed to His saints. To them God willed to make known what the riches of the glory of this mystery among the Gentiles are: WHICH IS CHRIST IN YOU, the hope of glory. Him (CHRIST) WE PREACH, warning every man and teaching every man in all wisdom, that we may PRESENT EVERY MAN PERFECT IN-CHRIST Jesus. To this end, I also labor, striving according to His working which works in me mightily.

"OUR MINISTRY IS TO REVEAL CHRIST IN US WHICH MAKES EVERY MAN PERFECT IN CHRIST" that is the Gospel Paul preached, and that is "the Gospel of Jesus Christ," of which is to save those who are lost and present them as perfect in CHRIST to God through His Righteousness.

Romans 10:9-10

[9]*If you declare with your mouth, "Jesus is Lord," and believe in your heart that God raised him from the dead, you will be saved.* [10]*For it is with your heart that you believe and are justified, and it is with your mouth that you profess your faith and are saved.*

John 12:47 (NKJV)

(If they don't obey I didn't come to Judge I come to Save)

⁴⁷*And if anyone hears My words and does not believe, I do not judge him; for I did not come to judge the world but to save the world.*

Galatians 1:6-8 (NKJV)

(Accursed to speak any other Gospel)

"I marvel that you are turning away so soon from Him who called you in the grace of Christ, to a different gospel, which is not another; but there are some who trouble you and want to pervert the gospel of Christ. But even if we, or an angel from heaven, preach any other gospel to you than what we have preached to you, let him be accursed."

Galatians 1:11-12 (NKJV)

(Gospel from Revelation of Christ)

"But I make known to you, brethren, that the gospel which was preached by me is not according to man. For I neither received it from man, nor was I taught it, but it came through the REVELATION of JESUS CHRIST."

Acts 20:24 (NKJV)

(GOSPEL of Grace came from Jesus for us to testify of)

But none of these things move me; nor do I count my life dear to myself, so that I may finish my race with joy, and the ministry which I received from the Lord Jesus, to testify to the gospel of the grace of God.

Galatians 1:15-16

(GOSPEL revealed is Christ in me)

But when it pleased God, who separated me from my mother's womb and called me through His grace, to REVEAL HIS SON (CHRIST) in ME, that I might preach Him (CHRIST) among the Gentiles, I did not immediately confer with flesh and blood,

Romans 1:16-17 (NKJV)

(In the Gospel of Christ, the Righteousness of God is revealed) For I am not ashamed of the gospel of Christ, for it is the power of God to salvation for everyone who believes, for the Jew first and also for the Greek. For in it the righteousness of God is revealed from faith to faith; as it is written, "The just shall live by faith."

All these readings portray the importance of the gospel of Christ in our lives as Christians. The works of Jesus on earth are revisited in the gospel, as well as the teachings of His disciples. We are encouraged to follow in His footsteps and to shun sin and the scribal law. Jesus came on earth not to judge us but to save us from our sins.

Our sins were, therefore, cleansed and the punishments which were prescribed by law for our sins were erased and replaced with promises of blessings. To claim these blessings, we are obliged to love one another and live in harmony. Love conquers the law because with love, no one will have the intentions to do something that will hurt or offend another person.

The questionnaire below will help you sum up all the sections we have covered through this book;:

1. What does this book pay special attention to?

2. Do you believe that the law was too stringent to follow?

3. What do you think should be done to improve the way Christians relate with each other as well as with other people around them?

4. How do you feel about forgiveness? Would you forgive someone who wronged you so badly that you were tempted to wish them bad?

Is the work you are doing for God being repaid in blessings or are you working in vain? Does your lifestyle allow God to recognize the work you are doing in His service? Remember that if you think you are serving God but not living from what Christ has done for you, then you are working in vain.

After completing the studying of this book, please share the important information contained in this book with others so that they too can claim and receive the blessings. If you find this book helpful, feel free to recommend it to someone else who might appreciate studying it too.

SO, I LEAVE YOU WITH SOME OF THE THINGS CHRIST HAS DONE FOR US.

Chapter 8
After the Cross

What are the Benefits that We Gain
from the Gospel of "Christ after the Cross?"

There are enormous benefits and blessings that you received from what JESUS did for you "After the Cross." Read each scripture below, and you will see JESUS was the reason for us having all of these blessings:

+ We are anointed by God (*2 Corinthians 1:21-22 NKJV*), so we can be free from the law (*Romans 10:4*).

+ We are justified in God's eyes through Jesus; *Galatians 2:26 NKJV*), so we can receive the *Righteousness* of God through Christ (*Romans 10:3; Romans 3:21-22; Romans 8:4 NKJV*); and be made righteous (right with God) in God's eyes.

+ We are Kings and Priest (*Revelation 1:5-6 NKJV*).

+ We have the Spiritual Blessings (*Ephesians 1:3 NKJV*)

+ We are adopted son's through Christ; (*Ephesians 1:4 NKJV*)

- God will supply our every need (*Philippians 4:19 NKJV*)

- He removed enmity between us and God which was caused by the law (*Ephesians 2: 15 NKJV*)

- He removed enmity from us through the Cross. *Ephesians 2:15-16 NKJV: "Having abolished in His flesh the enmity, that is, the law of commandments contained in ordinances, so as to create in Himself one new man from the two, thus making peace, and that He might reconcile them both to God in one body through the Cross, thereby putting to death the enmity."*

- We receive imputed righteousness (*Romans 4:6*).

- We are Abraham's seed through Christ and heirs to inheritance (*Galatians 3:29*).

- The Holy Spirit will live with us now and forever; *John 14:16*).

- We are forever forgiven (*Luke 7:48*).

- We are justified in God's sight (*Romans 5:1*).

- We are redeemed (*Revelation 5:9*).

- We get abounding Grace (*2 Corinthians 9:8*).

- We are ambassadors for Christ (*2 Corinthians 5:20 and Ephesians 6: 19-20*)

- Because the flesh was made weak by the law, Christ removed the law for us (*Romans 10:4 NKJV*)

- Because the law cannot make you righteousness with God;

- Christ made us Righteous (*Romans 10:4 NKJV*)

- You have been given Power (*Acts 1:8; Ephesians 2: 15*).

- Removed enmity and abolished the law of commandments (*Galatians 2:16*).

- So you would not be condemned (*Romans 8:1*).

- Christ redeemed us from curses (*Galatians 3:13*).

- So you can live free (*Romans 8:2*).

- So that all the promises of God gave us would be yes; (*2 Corinthians 1:20*).

- So that the blessings of Abraham will be ours (*Galatians 3:14*)

- So we can have Salvation apart from the law (*Romans 3:23-28; John 5:39-40*).

- So God will remember your sins and lawless deeds no more (*Hebrew 8:12*).

- So we can go into the Holy of Holies (*Hebrews 10:17-19*).

- So we can come boldly to the throne of Grace (*Hebrews 4:16*).

- Redeem us from all iniquity and purify us unto Himself (*Titus 2:14*).

- With Christ, I bear and bring forth much fruit (*John 5:4-5*).

- I am God's temple and He dwells in me (*1 Cor. 3:16*).

- We have received an anointing (*1 John 2:27*).

- We are Redeemed by Christ and our name will stay in the Lamb's Book of Life through him (*Revelation 21:27*).

- Christ canceled the written code that was against us on the Cross (*Colossians 2:14*).

- All our sins are forgiven by Christ's blood (*1 John 1:7*).

- Christ bore our sins on the Cross so that we can live (*1 Peter 2:4*).

- Adam puts us in sin; Christ takes us out of sin (*Romans 5:1719*).

- God adopts us because of Christ (*Ephesians 1:5*).

- We get an inheritance because of Christ (*Ephesians 1:11*).

- We become the sons of God because of Christ (*John 1:12*).

- We are heirs with Jesus (*Romans 8:17*)

- We are heavenly citizens (*2 Timothy 4:18*).

- We are Sanctified by Christ (*1 Corinthians 6:11*).

- We have a mansion in heaven (*John 14:2*).

- The Holy Spirit will live with us now and forever (*John 14:16*).

- We are indwelt by the Holy Spirit because of Christ (*Romans 8:9*).

- We are blessed with spiritual blessings because of Christ (*Ephesians 1:3*).

God shall supply our every need because of Christ (*Philippians 4:19*).

- **Christ** reconciled us back to God (*Romans 5: 10-11*).

- We are justified as a gift by GRACE through Christ (*Romans 3:24*).

- In Jesus the gift of *grace* and *righteousness* reign (*Romans 5:17 NKJV*).

To understand how this righteousness works in you and through Christ. You must first understand the *Grace* which reveals Christ to you, which comes through God's Grace.

- God calls you through *Grace* to reveal Jesus (*Galatians 1: 15-16 NLT*).

- *Grace* is a teacher (most people don't receive this revelation. So, they can't be taught by *Grace* to come into the understanding of Christ in me, or in other words, Christ in You.

- The Grace of God teaches you to say no to ungodly living (*Titus 2:11-13 NIV*).

He bore our sins in his body, so we can die to sin and live for righteousness. Now, we have returned to the Overseer of our souls (*1Peter 2: 24-25 NIV*).

- In the Gospel of Christ, the Righteousness of God is revealed (*Romans 1: 16-17 NKJV*).

The first Adam put us into sin. Through God's Grace he sent the second Adam to take us out of sin, so we can be made righteous and with God, forgiven through his blood sacrifice.

Romans 5:12-21 NLT:

(First Adam and second Adam (Christ) contrasted)

"12 When Adam sinned, sin entered the world. Adam's sin brought death, so death spread to everyone, for everyone sinned.

13 Yes, people sinned even before the law was given. But it was not counted as sin because there was not yet any law to break.

14 Still, everyone died—from the time of Adam to the time of Moses—even those who did not disobey an explicit commandment of God, as Adam did. Now Adam is a symbol, a representation of Christ, who was yet to come.

15 But there is a great difference between Adam's sin and God's gracious gift. For the sin of this one man, Adam, brought death to many. But even greater is God's wonderful grace and his gift of forgiveness to many through this other man, Jesus Christ.

¹⁶ And the result of God's gracious gift is very different from the result of that one man's sin. For Adam's sin led to condemnation, but God's free gift leads to our being made right with God, even though we are guilty of many sins.

¹⁷ For the sin of this one man, Adam, caused death to rule over many. But even greater is God's wonderful grace and his gift of righteousness, for all who receive it will live in triumph over sin and death through this one man, Jesus Christ.

¹⁸ Yes, Adam's one sin brings condemnation for everyone, but Christ's one act of righteousness brings a right relationship with God and new life for everyone.

¹⁹ Because one person disobeyed God, many became sinners. But because one other person obeyed God, many will be made righteous.

²⁰ God's law was given so that all people could see how sinful they were. But as people sinned more and more, God's wonderful grace became more abundant.

²¹ So just as sin ruled over all people and brought them to death, now God's wonderful grace rules instead, giving us right standing with God and resulting in eternal life through Jesus Christ our Lord."

www.ingramcontent.com/pod-product-compliance
Lightning Source LLC
Chambersburg PA
CBHW011216120626
46545CB00008B/3017